Caring Worship

Caring Worship

Helping Worship Leaders Provide Pastoral Care
through the Liturgy

HOWARD VANDERWELL

Foreword by John D. Witvliet

CASCADE *Books* · Eugene, Oregon

CARING WORSHIP
Helping Worship Leaders Provide Pastoral Care through the Liturgy

Cascade Books
An Imprint of Wipf and Stock Publishers
199 W. 8th Ave., Suite 3
Eugene, OR 97401

www.wipfandstock.com

PAPERBACK ISBN: 978-1-5326-1723-2
HARDCOVER ISBN: 978-1-4982-4179-3
EBOOK ISBN: 978-1-4982-4178-6

Cataloguing-in-Publication data:

Names: Vanderwell, Howard | Witvliet, John D., foreword writer.

Title: Caring worship : helping worship leaders provide pastoral care through the liturgy / Howard Vanderwell, with a foreword by John D. Witvliet.

Description: Eugene, OR: Cascade Books, 2017 | Includes bibliographical references.

Identifiers: ISBN 978-1-5326-1723-2 (paperback) | ISBN 978-1-4982-4179-3 (hardcover) | ISBN 978-1-4982-4178-6 (ebook)

Subjects: LCSH: Worship | Public worship—Planning | Ministers of music | Liturgics | Pastoral care

Classification: BV15 V152 2017 (paperback) | BV15 (ebook)

Manufactured in the U.S.A.   10/13/17

All Scripture quotations are taken from the Holy Bible New International Version NIV Copyright 1978, New York International Bible Society.

To
Norma deWaal Malefyt
My colleague in worship planning for nearly twenty years.
While we planned two worship liturgies each Wednesday
we wrestled with all the issues, taught each other, and enriched
the worship
for the eager worshipers at Hillcrest Church

Contents

Foreword

"As you stand before them, always love them."

When Howard Vanderwell received the distinguished alumni award from Calvin Theological Seminary in May 2017, he wrote a beautiful commendation to graduates that ended with this simple, but profound challenge. What a compelling and crucial invitation this is for everyone who has the privilege of preaching, presiding, praying, or leading music in Christian worship services.

"As you stand before them, always love them" is also an apt summary of the vision offered in this book. It is a vision that has emerged with passion and clarity throughout Rev. Vanderwell's years of service in Christian ministry. He has served as pastor of four congregations over a span of forty years, weaving together weekly preaching and worship leadership duties in both morning and evening Sunday services with weekday pastoral visits to nursing homes and hospitals, pastoral conversations with those preparing for marriage and those preparing for new church leadership roles, and pastoral leadership opportunities on councils, committees, and ministries within his own congregation and in a variety of significant denominational leadership roles. In all these ministry tasks, he learned increasingly to forge connections—to allow each weekday ministry activity to connect with the task of preaching and worship leadership, to engage in preaching and worship leadership as profoundly pastoral tasks.

Following these forty years, he has contributed for fifteen years now as a resource development specialist in our work at the Calvin Institute of Christian Worship, writing, teaching, advising, and serving as a mentor to a wide variety of ministry leaders—urging each of us to grow in our capacity as genuinely pastoral leaders whose service is marked by Christ-shaped love. For these fifteen years, I have been privileged to co-teach with him and to hear the stories that forged this deep pastoral vision in his own life. His own rich tapestry of ministry experiences and ministry advice could well be turned into a litany for seminary commencements or ordination services. I can almost hear it:

In winter and summer, "as you stand before them, always love them."

At baptism and funerals, "always love them."

As members come and as they go, "always love them."

In seasons of growth and seasons of pruning, "always love them."

In times of lament and in times of thanksgiving, "always love them."

In brand new churches and in established ones, "always love them."

In times of unity and in times of dissent, "always love them."

When you are young and when you are old, "always love them."

When they affirm you and even when they don't, "always love them."

When are you filled with energy and when you are fatigued, "always love them."

In life and in death, "always love them."

The more I have pondered this theme, the more it strikes me as a profound prophetic challenge to pastoral leaders today. So many discussions of church leadership invite us, often implicitly, to view our congregations in quite different ways—as problems to be solved, as a bundle of tensions to be managed, even as barriers to be overcome in the pursuit of some ministry dream. Too often discussions of worship or mission or leadership invite us, at least implicitly, to shape and lead a worship service beholden first to some evangelistic or liturgical or missional ideal, regardless of who is standing before us in the assembly, and the specific hopes and fears they bring with them to worship.

Into that world, Rev. Vanderwell's vision speaks a powerful word: "always love them."

With this in mind, what it would be like for all of us to meditate on 1 Corinthians 13 every time we prepare for leading worship? As we lead worship, how can we be "patient and kind, not envious or boastful or arrogant or rude," not "insisting on own way," nor being "irritable or resentful," never "rejoicing in wrongdoing, but rejoicing in the truth"?

To be sure, our love for those we lead must not be sentimental or simplistic. Loving those who we stand before does not mean giving them everything they want or dumbing down the message to gain high approval ratings. To the contrary, such love, cultivated through empathy, at times invites us to give voice to difficult themes and to convey warnings as well as comfort. Like wise parents, the posture here is one of a fierce, enduring love that seeks long-term flourishing for everyone as dearly loved children of God. It is a love that invites us to profound attentiveness to those with whom we serve, profound attentiveness to the spoken and unspoken fears and hopes that weave together in our daily lives.

Importantly, the vision explored here is not limited to human relationships. This is not merely about the love that pastoral worship leaders and preachers should cultivate toward their congregation—and the profound pastoral care that will emerge. More fully, this is about how pastoral leaders can learn to see, to savor, to celebrate, and ultimately to rest in the profound love of God that works through human relationality to embrace, nourish, and challenge us as we worship. In worship and through our lives, God is promising and blessing and speaking and convicting us. It is precisely in worship that we are invited to drink deeply of this awareness of God's love, and God's active and healing presence among us. Indeed, any healing or care that worship offers is not ultimately produced by the sole agency of a given leader, but rather by the Holy Spirit at work through us, alongside us, and—when necessary—in spite of us. This vision of the overflowing love of God is what makes ministry such a privilege and joy—even in the most challenging moments. We are called to love each other, ultimately, because God loves us first (1 John 4:7, 19). And thus this book offers a profoundly theocentric vision for how we can "walk in step with God's Spirit," participating in the remarkable, redemptive work of God to offer the kind of care we all so deeply long for.

So may God bless all who read of this book. Indeed, may God, according to the riches of divine glory, bless all who minister through worship and pastoral care, strengthening us in our inner being with power through the Holy Spirit, so that Jesus Christ may dwell deeply in our hearts through faith. In worship and in life together, may God's Spirit guide us to comprehend the breadth and length and height and depth of the love of Christ, so that we may be filled with all the fullness of God. To this triune God, who by the power at work within us is able to accomplish abundantly more than all we can ask or imagine—to this God be glory in the church and in Christ Jesus to all generations, forever and ever. Amen. (Based on Ephesians 3:14–21.)

John D. Witvliet
Calvin Institute of Christian Worship
Calvin College and Calvin Theological Seminary
June 2017

Preface

Those of us who worship regularly are privileged people. We are welcomed to come just as we are into the presence of God to meet with him. And those of us who are privileged to plan and lead worship stand in a sacred place—the place between God and his people when they meet together.

Those who come to worship are participating in a noble service, and they deserve to be served well and never disappointed. And those who serve together as the planners and the leaders of a worship service carry a large responsibility to the worshiping community and also to God. As they craft a worship liturgy, they must be conscious of how important their task is. What they plan, the thought they put into it, and the manner in which they lead will determine how engaging this worship encounter will be. Some elements of worship carry the power to bless quite aside from the role of planners and leaders. Yet even at such times, the caring that is experienced will be greatly enhanced when worship is planned and led well. Consequently, the movement toward including a wide range of lay leaders in worship should also include a concern for the training they have for such a task. Some may be adequately trained for such a leadership role, but it may be new to some others of them. How able they are to handle such responsibilities will either aid worship or hinder it.

So these materials have those two groups of people in mind—those who work together in designing and planning a worship service, and those, clergy or lay, who serve together in leading the worship services. Both of these groups are found in virtually all churches, regardless of size, style, or pattern of worship. The insights we provide here are valid for all leaders, clergy and lay, those who plan and design and those who lead. And these insights are equally valid for all churches, regardless of whether the Sunday morning worshipers number fifty-five or fifteen hundred, regardless of whether their worship is carefully structured according to a liturgy such as the *Book of Common Prayer* or is contemporary and more informal.

Maybe you are one of those who works with others to plan worship services. Maybe you lead services. Maybe you are a pastor or a musician. Whatever your role, you probably realize that you have to deal with many expectations, pressures, and a wide range of possibilities. I've been there with you for many years in a number of different congregations, and now I continue that work through the Calvin Institute of Christian Worship.

Because worship leadership is such a key spot to be in, I think we need to talk together about some of what goes into our work. So I eagerly provide these insights on some of the issues worship planners and leaders face as I've come to know them. I hope it will encourage you, inform you, keep you fresh, and make you a greater blessing to the folks you lead each week.

This book is not primarily concerned with how to plan worship, or the issues of worship, or how to structure the liturgy. I assume you will learn that in other places. I'm convinced that the liturgies we plan and lead should be a special source of excellent pastoral care, and that is my focus here. This material aims to increase our understanding of the potentially pastoral nature of a liturgy that is conducted sensitively.

Some insights come slowly in the life of the church. For instance, a careful study of church history reveals to us that some key doctrines of the church were not clarified until a number of generations had passed. It took a number of years before the church agreed on which books should be included in the canon of Scripture. Not until almost the fourth century was the doctrine of the Trinity and the interrelationship of the three persons of the

Trinity clarified. It took until the twentieth century to more carefully define the work of the Holy Spirit.

Similarly, the church's convictions about its worship have also unfolded slowly. While in early centuries the church shaped its worship around a four-fold pattern of gathering-word-response-dismissal, those concepts have gone through much refinement since that time. But perhaps the most thorough re-examining of worship began approximately fifty years ago. In 1962 the Second Vatican Council set the stage for worship renewal, first in Roman Catholicism, and later beyond Catholicism. Soon the desire for worship renewal spread to nearly all churches like ripples in a pond.

Awareness of how caring a liturgy can be hasn't always been clear in the mind of many. In my seminary training in the 1960s, only two courses treated worship theology. Homiletics taught us the history, theory, and practice of sermon writing. And liturgics gave us instruction in the history and theory of the worship service. Looking back, I realize we only skimmed the surface of such subjects.

A third course called poimenics focused on the history, principles, and practice of pastoral care. The whole concept of pastoral care was only in its infancy at that time. We were advised that pastoral care could be accomplished in several ways: by pastoral calling on the sick and shut-ins, visitation of families in their homes to assess their needs and give supportive encouragement, and through corrective one-on-one counsel to those who were erring.

Yet pastoral care was completely separated from worship. In worship courses no hint ever surfaced that pastoral care might be provided in the context of worship. In the courses on pastoral care, no one imagined that it might be accomplished in a worship service. So pastoral care and worship were strangers who never met and courted.

Gradually, in the twentieth century, a new awareness emerged of the potential for providing pastoral care during the liturgy. It began slowly. Many new questions about worship were arising. Is it wise to sing only historic hymns? Should we include more contemporary songs? Is a service of confession necessary every week? How personal should the prayers of the people be? What musical instruments are best for accompaniment? Should we incorporate more creativity? Should the church have more lay leadership in worship? Should we return to more ancient patterns or more contemporary forms of worship? What kind of vocabulary should worship leaders use? The questions and discussions continued. We called it worship renewal, although this was a time that brought both divisive conflict and renewed vitality in worship.

In the middle of such questioning and reevaluation, and among all the other worship issues that were on the table, the development of pastoral care ministries was also taking place. At first worship and pastoral care were quite separate, but gradually the two were joined in the mind of many and the possibility of providing greater pastoral care during the liturgy developed. Up until that time, most pastoral care was envisioned as taking place outside of the weekly worship service, generally in homes. Only gradually has the possibility of providing such care within the liturgy begun to develop. Our focus here is on that unfolding.

The need for expanding our expectations for the liturgy became apparent when John H. Westerhoff III and Gwen Kennedy Nevil claimed in 1978 that our rituals shape and form us in fundamental ways. Part of this formation has to do with learning. Much of that learning was associated with preaching. They claim, however, "Liturgy and learning have been linked since the birth of the Christian era, but of late they have become estranged."[1] And yet their emphasis continued to be on learning, more than giving and receiving pastoral care. If learning is essential and if the liturgy can encourage learning, then surely the liturgy can provide necessary pastoral care for those who come with their hurts.

Though evangelicals found it difficult to trust liberal voices, Harry Emerson Fosdick stirred the concern of many by insisting that preaching was to be personal counseling on a group scale. His voice, combined with others who followed him, opened up both the sermon and eventually the liturgy to broader purposes that

1. Neville and Westerhoff, *Learning through Liturgy*, 91.

would better form those who had come to worship. The result of this increased awareness moved the church toward the expression of more formative care for the worshiper.

So, gradually the church doors were opening to a new and growing emphasis—that the function of preaching is more than the communication of knowledge and truth. That is, its function is not primarily a cognitive one, but one that also has some concern for worshipers' need for pastoral care and counseling.

Yet this movement within the church still did not embody a clear conviction that the liturgy, aside from the sermon, has power to provide the care needed. That next step was still be to be taken. Liturgy was still seen as something secondary, preliminary, and perhaps preparatory, to the preaching. Any further steps that would embrace liturgy as the source of meaningful pastoral care would have to wait for some other, perhaps yet unknown, influences that were still in the process of developing. I hope that the material provided here will serve that cause.

I know that some who study worship are uneasy with this new emphasis. They are suspicious that it focuses worshipers more on the horizontal and less on the vertical—more on us and less on God. Worship is not, first of all, for us, they plead. And that shift in focus could indeed be a risk. Worship is first of all a dialogic encounter with God. But as we worship, the needs of those who worship also receive consideration. As a matter of fact, the more God-centered our worship is, the greater is its power to care for us and meet the personal needs we bring with us.

Our purpose here is to underscore a developing awareness of how the liturgy can serve the cause of caring for souls. This seems reasonable. When we experience the astonishment of encountering a God who listens, hears, and answers, even when we have wounded and offended him by our rejection and disobedience, surely we will experience his care and healing.

So as you read and reflect on this material, join the process of increasingly bringing together the liturgy and the care of souls. Your worship will be richer, spiritual formation will take place more naturally, and your congregation will be served well.

Introduction

On a recent Sunday morning, I worshiped in a way that fed my soul and healed my spirit in an unusual manner. It illustrates what I mean by "caring worship."

First I must tell you what my life involved in the week before that Sunday morning. I came to worship that Sunday morning with a special set of needs, not entirely different from the kinds of needs with which many worshipers come. Early that week I experienced some health problems that didn't seem severe, yet they seemed too significant to ignore. After seeking a consultation with my doctor, his advice was that I should be checked into the hospital for a battery of tests to discern the cause and its potential severity. That check-in began a five-day hospitalization that involved probing, examining, and testing of every imaginable kind. It was a far different week from what I anticipated, and frankly, distressing to me.

I'm thankful the outcome was not a critical diagnosis. Nevertheless, I was told that I'd suffered a small stroke. The word "small" can be deceiving. Any such news is disconcerting. I'm grateful that the reports indicate the damage was minimal and all was detected early. But what did happen is that I encountered many thoughts, feelings, and emotions I had never anticipated the week would involve. While I had previously considered myself healthy, now I felt terribly fragile. While I had felt strong, now I felt vulnerable. A few days ago I was enjoying an active life, with plans for more, and now I was set aside in a hospital room while the rest of the world went on by. My composure gave way to sadness and tears. A pervading sense of uncertainty and doubt swept over me. Even after I was able to return home Friday evening with the news, "It's not serious, but it will take some care," this sadness, sense of fragility, and doubt continued to hang over me. It was, to be sure, a high-anxiety experience.

I went to worship Sunday morning, not just because it's my custom to do so. I went because I sensed deep within me the need to be in the presence of God and with his people. I was weak and distracted. A week in the hospital had done its work, causing me to lose the strength of my faith. I knew it would be good for my painfully bruised spirit, and it didn't take long before my need was greatly satisfied.

Perhaps it was because I came to that service with such a needy heart, or with an extra thirsty spirit, or a greater readiness to receive what was offered, but what happened to me in that worship time typifies what I believe should happen regularly all over the world, Sunday after Sunday. In this worship experience I felt immensely cared for. I have always found the sermons that our pastor preaches to be thoughtful, insightful, nurturing to my spirit. This week was no different. But what captured my heart this week was the liturgy.

- As I entered the sanctuary I became conscious of being in a holy place. The beauty of the sanctuary, the messages from the stained-glass windows, the quiet, the sense of expectancy that I felt as I entered all spoke to me in a comforting way. "This place is so different from your hospital room," they said. "This place is holy and God dwells here."

- As I walked down the aisle I heard that the organist was playing "I Am the Bread of Life." Its familiar words began rolling through my mind, I hummed it as I walked to my pew.

- When the congregation sang the first hymn, I heard more familiar and beloved words: "Praise, my soul, the king of heaven." But this time a phrase caught my attention in a new way. We sang ". . . in his hand he gently bears us, rescues us from all our foes." "That's me," I said to myself. "I have been rescued this week from a more serious diagnosis that I feared." God was reminding me that he was at work.

- And then the pastor raised her arms and said that God Almighty, Father, Son, and Holy Spirit greeted us with "grace, mercy and peace." They were words I'd heard so often, but this time if felt like God reached right over to the pew where I was standing, put his arm around me, and said, "Howard, it's so good to see you here this morning. We need to be together!" I cried inside.

- In the pastoral prayer I heard the pastor talk to the Lord about people who have found "the veil between this life and the next one prove to be thin and need to trust your gracious faithfulness." Had she really looked right into my heart?

- But after the sermon, all my brothers and sisters here joined me in singing, "Jesus draw me ever nearer as I labor through the storm." And then our spirits became even more intense when we sang the refrain, "May this journey bring a blessing; may I rise on wings of faith and at the end of my heart's testing, with your likeness let me wake."[1]

- And then the best of all happened. We were about to leave after a full hour of riches from God's hand. And the preaching pastor raised his arms and promised us, "The Lord bless you and keep you; the Lord make his face to shine on you and be gracious to you; the Lord turn his face toward you and give you peace." The Lord would be going with me! That precious benediction meant more to me that morning than ever before. Never alone. After feeling such aloneness this week, here was the corrective truth: Never Alone.

As I reflected on my experiences that Sunday morning, I came to realize that this was a regular Sunday morning service. There were no unusual elements in that service. The same elements were probably present this week as had been many other weeks.

1. "Jesus, Draw Me Ever Nearer," Margaret Becker and Keith Getty, 2001, Modern M Music.

So what made the difference? I did. My state of mind and heart made the difference. I came with an acute awareness of how needy I was, and I listened more carefully that morning. I picked up gems that had probably been present many weeks before but that I had not noticed. Those who lead our worship have generally been in tune with our needs and intent on caring well for us. This week, however, I noticed and picked the fruit they had made available.

HOW TO USE THESE MATERIALS

My aim in this book is not merely to provide information for you, but to upgrade your worship leadership skills and to improve the benefits that your congregation receives in worship. In case you have opportunity to examine these ideas with others, I'm including a few questions at the end of each chapter to guide you in some further thought on the matter.

I suggest the following ways to use these resources to bring fruit in a worshiping congregation. I encourage you to think of others as well.

1. *Personal Study.* This thoughtful and provocative material can be used in personal study. Pastors, directors of worship ministries, worship planners, church elders, teachers, worship committees, and any others associated with the worship life of the congregation will certainly benefit by personally studying this material. In addition, making this material available as a resource for study by worshiping members will increase the thoughtfulness of such worshipers.

2. *Small Group Study.* Greater benefit comes when small groups study material like this together and engage in discussion and evaluation with a healthy interchange of ideas. Twenty to thirty minutes at the beginning of a planning meeting will prove to be a valuable investment.

   • A worship planning team can discuss one of the short chapters each time they meet to plan a worship service.

- Members of a worship committee who are responsible for overseeing the worship life of the congregation could devote time at their regular meetings to increase their knowledge of worship issues and their awareness of the worship life of their congregation by discussing a chapter in each meeting.

- Church elders who are responsible for the spiritual health of the congregation would do well to take a short period of time at their monthly meeting to discuss a chapter of this material.

3. *Educational Groups.* Adult education groups, Sunday school groups, or any group gathered to study worship will find these materials to be a helpful guide. They can do this either in a class setting or on a retreat.

4. *Students.* Those who are seeking an education with an eye to leadership in the worship life of the congregation will find that this material provides a perspective on worship planning and worship leadership that can raise their ministry to a higher level.

PART ONE

Perspectives on Worshipping

The first section of this material takes us behind the scenes of a worship service and asks some basic questions about what is happening, who is involved, and what hopes are present. Much of this deals with matters that do not normally meet the eye, yet they are key to the entire endeavor of worship. These are the foundational questions for getting started:

- What is the nature of a worship service?
- What is the purpose of worship?
- Why do worship services follow a liturgy?
- What is the nature and condition of the people who come to worship?
- What is required to be an effective worship leader?

Chapter 1

When the Needy Come to Church

Much of my professional life has been spent in the pastorate—four congregations over forty years. That means that nearly every Sunday I led a congregation in worship, usually twice each Sunday.

While serving in those pastorates, I always watched the worshipers as they arrived each Sunday. I could see them out of my study window, and I watched them carefully. It was part of my preparation for leading worship. Once the service began, I continued to survey them from my vantage point on the platform. As their pastor, I knew most of these folks pretty well. And I knew much of what they were bringing with them to church. They looked so "put together"—dressed up, nice families, polite and friendly. Of course, some had visible, physical challenges. One used a walker; another, a wheelchair. Someone else was blind, and a young lady had some cognitive challenges.

But I knew most of them inside, too, and I knew that view was different. Nearly all of them were experiencing some form or degree of brokenness. Some came with needs that were not so visible—a troubled marriage, a divorce, a young lady who was unmarried and disappointed, a grieving widow, a young man who dealt with depression, one who sat apart, seemingly unable to relate to others, another with addictions, some others who'd lost their sense of direction in life, and parents who grieved their children's spiritual condition.

But still other needs were private, shared with no one. Some were doubting the faith; some wondered about the existence of God; some were riddled with guilt or crippled by anxiety, self-doubts, or anger. A few were victims of abuse, and I knew several children who were frightened. Still others' needs were unknown, for they'd just dropped in as visitors.

What a variety! And what an intense gathering of needs were present in church as worship began. Soon a knot developed in my stomach and pulled so tightly that I thought it was going to strangle me. "Maybe it's easier just not to think about such things," a little voice inside whispers. And yet . . . they have come with the hope of receiving something that will help them

> "When I sit on the podium and survey those who have come to worship, with my mind's eye I see that 70 percent of them are holding up a little white flag with the red letters H-E-L-P on it."
>
> —John R. W. Stott, Address at the Congress on Biblical Exposition, 1985.

carry on for another week. They've come looking for something that would at least restore some degree of *hope*. Their hope lies in being lifted to another world, beyond the pain and disillusionment of this fallen and broken world, to the world where all is right and righteous, where there is comfort and care, healing and renewal. Their eyes need to be lifted to a vision of God and his throne. I began to ask myself, "How is this liturgy that we've planned going to accomplish what they've come expecting? Should we maybe have planned it more thoughtfully?"

I've spent time with some of them in their homes talking things through and praying with them. I've met them in their hospital room and encouraged them. And a number of them have been in my office for some heart-to-heart counsel. Others have gone to a professional counselor with their needs, obviously more than a pastor can handle. Still others have turned to friends or their Stephen Minister in church for some encouragement and support. But many others have seen no one and have shared their needs with no one. They are alone. And now here they are, expecting something to happen, someone to connect with. This worship service may be their only hope this morning (or even this week), though they perhaps haven't even been willing to admit that to themselves.

Again the Holy Spirit speaks to my heart: "This is the time for pastoral care!" And my heart answers, "Really, Lord? Here? Now? Where in this hour do you hope to do that?"

Too often most of the attention has focused on the sermon and its work. The sermon, we are taught, must make the difference. Many words have been spoken, books written, and conferences held about the sermon—how to write it and preach it. Among other things, we are told it must be relevant. In other words, the sermon has to care for needy worshipers. The truth is that sermons can indeed make a big difference for worshipers, but even the best of preachers will admit that we're simply requiring too much from a sermon if we expect it to do all the work of pastoral care. How much better if there is a synergy of caring between the sermon and the liturgy. So, we need to shift our attention toward the liturgy as a companion to the preached word.

> "When [Jesus] saw the crowds he had compassion on them, because they were harassed and helpless, like sheep without a shepherd."
>
> —Matthew 9:36

Some folks are not fond of the word, but *liturgy* means the "order of the service" or the "acts of worship." In other words, everything that happens between the time you arrive and the time you leave is liturgy. It may be formal or informal, spontaneous or carefully structured, the same every week or different each time, but it's the liturgy. Some traditions put a lot of emphasis on a carefully structured liturgy and others do their best to avoid looking like they are "liturgical."

Wise is the church that takes a fresh look at the powerful potential for caring for worshipers' needs through the liturgy, no longer looking at it as merely a "warm-up" for the main event, the sermon. No longer may we allow ourselves as worship planners the liberty of hastily piecing the liturgy together. The pastor and worship planners must together give careful attention to every element of the service. Liturgy has power—more power than most churches acknowledge. It's critical to think about how pastoral care can be provided for the concerns of worshipers—when they sit together, receive God's greeting, pass the peace to one another, pray together, receive the assurance of pardon, sing together, celebrate the sacraments, and read the Bible. All of these have the power to bless those who desperately need such a blessing! These elements of worship are not so many preliminary steps before we get to the sermon, but are rather events that are pregnant with the possibility of expressing care and conveying healing. Worshipers have a right to expect the entire worship service to provide care for them.

TO PONDER AND DISCUSS

1. When you hear the word "liturgy," what comes to mind?

2. How much effort and attention do you, and your worship planners, put into the liturgy compared to the sermon? What does that say about your expectations?

3. Have you personally experienced the caring and healing power of the liturgy in worship? If so, how did it come? How did it affect you?

4. How intentional are most worshipers and worship planners about such caring? How can we improve that?

Chapter 2

Needs in Every Pew

L et's follow through a bit more on the idea that worshipers bring their needs to church and let's examine what types of needs are usually present.

During those years when I served in the pastorate, for the most part I saw the same people before me week after week. I generally preached about forty-five Sundays annually. My fourth pastorate was a long one, and after a while I came to consider members of the congregation "my people." That meant that when a worship service began, I had a pretty good knowledge of who they were, their history as a group, their perspective on most things, and what their needs were individually and as a congregation. True, sometimes they surprised me, but not often. And that also meant that at any point in the liturgy or the sermon, I had a pretty good feel for how they were receiving what I was saying and whether it resonated with them or not.

I don't serve in a pastorate anymore, yet I still preach. I'm one of those "guest preachers" who comes to "fill a pulpit." Sometimes my role involves only preaching the sermon, sometimes also leading the liturgy. Over a period of weeks I may be serving in congregations that are different in nature from one another. Yet they all have one thing in common: the people I am leading are usually strangers to me. I have no pastoral tie with them. I don't really "know" them. And yet I need to lead them.

When I first left the pastorate and began preaching as a guest, I found preaching to be a distressing experience. How could I meaningfully lead people I didn't really know? I realized more than ever how I had relied on my knowledge of my parishioners to make my leadership of the liturgy relevant to my hearers' personal needs, though I wasn't usually conscious of that. I found leading people who were strangers to me frustrating and unfulfilling, and I longed for my own pastorate again. Over time I did get past that barrier and told myself that my task was to bring the truth faithfully and let the Holy Spirit do what he wants with it, applying it as each may need it.

Then gradually a new awareness set in—one that I probably should have had all along: all people are much the same in many respects. There are common human needs that I may assume, even if I do not have personal information about each person. No worshiper is totally whole. (Only those who are around the throne in heaven are whole!) All others come with varying degrees of brokenness. The Bible uses many different terms

> "Come to me, all you who are weary and burdened, and I will give you rest. Take my yoke upon you and learn from me for I am gentle and humble in heart, and you will find rest for your souls. For my yoke is easy and my burden is light."
>
> —Matthew 11:28–30

to point to the experience of human brokenness. Psalm 42 speaks of a soul that is downcast and disturbed. Psalm 73 speaks of those whose hearts are grieved and whose spirits are embittered. Isaiah 40 refers to those who grow tired and weary. Jesus calls to himself those who are weary and burdened (Matt 11:28). At another time, Jesus saw that the crowds were harassed and helpless, like sheep without a shepherd (Matt 9:36). These are only examples of the different forms of neediness that worshipers may be experiencing.

An awareness of such common human needs ought to be in the mind of all of us who are worship planners, worship leaders, and preachers. That means, of course, that those who will serve best in any of those capacities are students of human nature and observe what is happening to people. There are many common human needs, but let me suggest nine that I find are of particular concern when we come to worship. You can perhaps identify others in addition to these.

1. *The need for instruction in truth.* We are bombarded weekly by thousands of messages about what to believe and how to live. Often these prove to be terribly confusing. This cacophony of confusing voices leaves us wondering what is true, what we are to believe, and in which direction we should go. Is there unchanging, always-reliable truth?

2. *The need for grace.* Many of our needs in some way are caused by and related to the fact that we are people who fail, stumble, and disappoint God, others near us, and ourselves. So one of the most fundamental needs we have is the need to know that God loves us in spite of ourselves. Such grace is at the heart of the Christian gospel, and therefore we might say that the foundational need is for the gospel of Christ.

3. *The need for hope.* It has been said that we can live only a few minutes without air, but we cannot live at all without hope. When our world seems so violent and broken, we ask if there is hope for any change. When our health deteriorates, we look for some hope of healing. When relationships fracture, we beg for some hope of reconciliation. When our failures crush us, we look for hope to restart again. When our marriages and family crumble, we wonder about hope for a new start. When our dreams are dashed, we seek for some hope to dream again. One of the most fundamental gifts worship can give is the gift of hope.

4. *The need for acceptance and affirmation.* We seek this in all our relationships, including in our relationship with God. A visitor to worship wonders if it's OK to come as a stranger. Even a long-time member still has times of needing the assurance that others accept him or her. Perhaps all of us at some time or other hear this little internal voice whispering,

"Do these other people accept me as part of the group?" We may even wonder if God accepts us. Does he notice me here? Am I worthy to come? Adolescents can experience that need quite strongly.

5. *The need for reconciliation.* It's pretty safe to say that every worshiper on some level experiences stress fractures in relationships. It may be within the marriage or family circle, with friends/coworkers, and even in church relationships. But we also face the matter of reconciliation with God. Fractures produce feelings of shame, guilt, and pain. So as we come to worship the question is present, what can possibly erase the offense and the distance between us? Is there something here that will help us be reconciled to one another?

6. *The need to know of God's presence with me.* Loneliness commonly haunts all of us, especially a God-loneliness. And so some come to worship needing to experience the presence of God again. They find it easier to experience that presence in the quiet of a sanctuary with the visual reminders around them. Even when they prepare to leave and go back to the ups and downs of life again, they begin asking "Will he be with me there? Does God, in fact, go with me?" Is there something here to reassure me of that?

7. *The need for a healthy identity.* All of us at one time or another find that achieving a healthy sense of identity is one of the most challenging tasks of life. Children and adolescents struggle with it. Middle adults and senior adults are asking themselves the same questions they asked in adolescence—Who am I? What am I worth? And what am I here for? Every time something occurs that changes our circumstances in life, the same search comes up all over again.

8. *The need to trust God when times are tough.* Scattered throughout the congregation are people who once trusted God, but for whom life has been hard and times have been tough. Now when they most need to trust God they are least able to do so. Everything within them seems to shout "No!" at

the thought of trusting God right now. So they come hungry for something more than another exhortation to trust God. They are looking for the assurance that God is trustworthy and it is OK to trust him even when the going is hard and much of life is mysterious.

9. *The need for prayer.* It's usually hard for us to admit to each other that we find it hard to pray. Yet many of us do. We are stunned by the events of life or traumatized by bad news, and prayer just doesn't come. So we come to worship needing somebody to talk to God for us, or teach us to pray again. Or perhaps we need a safe place to pray by ourselves.

You may think of other types of needs. And you may find that some of these are more apparent than others. Several things about people's needs become clear: the worshipers who gather are a needy group, their needs take many different forms, and it is unacceptable to ignore them. Yet it is also unreasonable to expect that the sermon is able to effectively address all these needs. We should be eager, therefore, to engage the worshipers in a liturgy that is sensitive to such concerns and able to communicate caring.

> "The kingdom of heaven is like a man who sowed good seed in his field. But while everyone was sleeping his enemy came and sowed weeds among the wheat, and went away. When the wheat sprouted and formed heads, then the weeds also appeared."
>
> —Matthew 13:24–26

TO PONDER AND DISCUSS

1. Review the needs that were presented above. What are the greatest needs in your congregation? How might they be addressed in worship?

2. Is it really necessary to know the needs of worshipers? How can we relinquish this task to the Holy Spirit in applying the truth as he wants?

3. In what way has your knowledge, or lack of knowledge, of the needs of worshipers shaped how you have planned or lead a liturgy?

4. Cite two or three elements of the liturgy this past week that were specifically designed to meet the needs of worshipers. What were the needs you had in mind, and what response were you expecting?

Chapter 3

More Than a Sermon

I HOPE THAT BY now you've caught an idea of what I have in mind for these pages. We are colleagues who stand together in that sacred spot where God and his people meet. The two of them desire to be in conversation with each other and we are called to facilitate that conversation. It's a sacred place. Our goal, therefore, is to facilitate that interaction between God and his people *so that* they experience God's loving care for them in their neediness. One of our major goals in all of ministry is to provide thoughtful pastoral care. My aim here is to demonstrate that *worship leaders can* provide thoughtful pastoral care and to help you do so meaningfully.

Perhaps it's a bit risky to use the word *liturgy* for it can easily be misunderstood. Some recoil at the word, quite uncertain about what the term refers to, for they don't think of their worship as liturgical. Others are puzzled by the word because when they move from one congregation to another, one of the first things they notice is how different the worship services are. Some are highly structured, with a large number of rather formal actions, and the structure seems to remain the same every week. Others have a liturgy that seems simple, yet with significant variety—an opening, a time of singing, and a sermon. Some churches print a detailed liturgy for worshipers to follow, others do not. Some seem rather informal and spontaneous. Some are "high church," some are "low church." But regardless of the form, it is "liturgy." So liturgy looks different from one church to another, yet it's important to understand that *every* church has a liturgy, whether they use the term or not.

In some traditions, all attention is focused on the sermon. Folks will talk about going to church as "going to sermon," as though the worship service is a sermon and little else. When churches advertise their services, they'll usually give only the sermon title. And if you ask someone, "How was church this morning?" they'll likely tell you something the pastor preached about. True, the sermon often takes up the largest single block of time in a worship service, and a pastor often spends more time on the sermon than on any other part of the service, but maybe we have overemphasized it. Is there nothing else? Could worship be more than a sermon? That is not to diminish the significance of the sermon, but to point out the sermon does not stand alone.

Other readers may be familiar with what liturgy involves but have a somewhat negative reaction because they've been taught, "Our church doesn't have a liturgy like that; that's what high churches, more formal churches, have." Others might resist the term because they think of liturgy as somewhat rigid, and they desire worship that is more spontaneous and informal.

So what is liturgy, and do all churches have it?

In short, liturgy is the form or structure of the entire worship service. I've said previously that it's everything that happens from the time you arrive until the time you leave. Some prefer

> The basic and rudimentary shape of worship has historically been fourfold:
>
> The Gathering
> The Word of God
> The Table of the Lord
> The Sending
>
> Each of these four parts includes a variety of elements, such as prayers, hymns, acclamations, testimonials, and responses.
>
> —From Robert Webber, *Worship Is a Verb*, 49–59.

to think of it as everything that surrounds the sermon. Literally it is the "work of the people."

Generally, worship services are composed of several clearly defined parts. Some prefer to speak of four elements: the music and song, the spoken liturgy, the sermon, and the sacraments. Others will prefer to speak of three parts: the sermon, the sacraments, and the liturgy (in both word and song). Either way, if we came for a sermon only and left immediately after the sermon was finished, we would have no liturgy. But no worship service consists of only a sermon. So we might say that liturgy is the work of the people in the worship service, while the sermon is the work of the preacher. Therefore, all churches have a liturgy, though it may take various forms.

Once we have recognized that there is a liturgy in a worship service, we must develop some clear ideas of just what its purpose is. Some prefer to see the liturgy as the part of the service in which musicians have an opportunity to inspire worshipers, often leading to an overemphasis on musicians and their performance. Others call the liturgy the "preliminaries" that set the stage for the sermon. Such a perspective can lead to a utilitarian concept of the liturgy.

But liturgy receives its highest value when it is recognized as the forum in which the worshipers encounter God. The liturgy, therefore, facilitates the dialog between God and his people. God's words and acts are remembered and responded to in faith. Consequently the liturgy becomes those actions in which worshipers, with all their cares and concerns, become engaged in a dialog that involves direct engagement with the Father, the Son, and the Holy Spirit.

There is ample evidence in early church history that the liturgy followed a general four-fold pattern. A church is wise to follow this historical pattern to safeguard its worship as a dialog with God.

- *The Gathering*—The meeting with God begins. God welcomes us into his presence. The beginning of our engagement with him will usually include such actions as receiving his peace, singing our praise and adoration, confessing our sins, receiving his pardon, and offering our prayers.

- *The Word of God*—God's voice comes to us primarily through his Word, so it follows that Scripture readings will have a prominent place in a Christian worship service. There should be multiple readings, often selected on the basis of the theme of the service, the events of the week, or the portion of the Christian Year being observed. One of the major elements of the liturgy is the reading of the Word and the sermon, which explains and applies that Word for the worshipers.

- *Response to the Word*—In early practice, and still in many churches today, this response took the form of the weekly celebration of the Lord's Supper. As an act of faith, those who hear God's voice through the Word gather at the Lord's Table to remember his gift of salvation. Over the centuries, some traditions have chosen to invite worshipers to come to the Table less frequently (monthly or quarterly). Regardless of the frequency of the Lord's Supper, congregations will respond with affirmations of faith, songs of commitment, offerings of gratitude, and prayers.

- *Sending*—After God and his people have engaged in their conversation together, and worshipers have heard God's Word and responded in faith, the people are sent forth to serve. So the dismissal will likely include a benedictory blessing, words of sending, and a song of faith and commitment.

We encourage worship planners to take this four-fold pattern into consideration when they choose or create a liturgy. We encourage you to take a look at your worship services with that in mind. Liturgy is not an exercise we go through to win the favor of God, nor is it a pep-rally for the faithful. It is not a concert or program, and it's not intended to be a therapy session. A church may implement this pattern according to its own tradition and culture, but such a pattern certainly should undergird liturgy as a safeguard to retain the conviction that worship is a dialog with God. When God's people engage in conversation with God, you can expect things to happen. The people will hear God's word and be strengthened in their faith by remembering his actions and promises. Through worship, they can find their way if they have lost it. They can be assured of his grace and his presence. They will find help and healing for their wounds, and certainty for their doubts. They can live with a clearer view of God's presence with them and his mission for them.

> "And let us consider how we may spur one another on toward love and good deeds. Let us not give up meeting together, as some are in the habit of doing, but let us encourage one another—and all the more as you see the Day approaching."
>
> —Hebrews 10:24–25

So now we see that what is constructed to implement this pattern, regardless of how simple or elaborate, is the "liturgy." And those who lead it are "liturgists."

We believe the liturgy *is* worship, regardless of how simple or elaborate. It is through the liturgy that we engage with God. His voice should come through clearly, and our response should be just as clear. Consequently, worship should be planned carefully and thoughtfully. And those who lead it, as liturgists, should reflect a careful and thoughtful spirit.

TO PONDER AND DISCUSS

1. Are you comfortable with the underlying four-fold pattern of worship—Gathering, Word, Response, Sending? Examine a recent worship service, and point out where each of these four elements is found and what it includes.

2. If the liturgy has an intrinsic value of its own, how should worship planners approach their task? Find three words that would best describe how their work ought to be done.

3. How does this explanation of the value of the liturgy compare with what your congregation's worship leaders have usually thought? Are there corrections that need to be made? Where

might they be made? How could that conversation be opened up?

Chapter 4

It's Not about You, or Maybe It Is!

I THINK YOU'VE PROBABLY heard that cry, often with a hint of rebuke in it: "It's not about you!" It's a good reminder in this age of individualism in which most of us do think it's all about us!

But when we ask that question about worship, we just may come out in a different spot from the one we expected. I think we will come out saying, on the one hand, it's not all about us; and on the other hand, we will find ourselves saying that it is at least somewhat about us. Yes and no. Can that be? Let me explain.

This of course leads us into a consideration of the purpose of worship. Why do we worship? What is the purpose? How are we to evaluate it? When we ask these questions, we find that people can have a variety of legitimate expectations for Christian worship.

"Carlyle Marney, my late colleague who once taught future pastors with me here at Duke, was fond of saying something to the effect that 'our worship has to do with who God is, but it also has to do with who we are and who we wish to God we were'!"

—William Willimon, *Worship as Pastoral Care*, 13.

Many scholars trace the word "worship" back to its Old English roots, *weorthscipe*, "the state of being worthy or honorable" or "worthiness." In the 1300s, people also began using the word as a verb—to honor. The purpose of worship

24

is to declare the *worth* of God, to respond with awe and reverence to him as the most holy One. We agree that this is to be the primary purpose of all worship, even all of life. Paul exhorts us, "Whatever you do, do it all to the glory of God" (1 Cor 10:31). John, in Revelation 4 and 5, describes his vision of the throne room in heaven and the sovereign Lord seated on the throne. There, four living creatures and twenty-four elders (the angels and the church) are always ascribing praise, honor, glory, and power to the one on the throne. The heart of worship is to respond to God's glory in a way he deserves. And so if you ask some of your worshipers why they came to worship they will say, "We came to give God honor and glory."

If giving God glory is the fundamental activity of worship, we must proceed to another question. What shall we do in worship that will properly give him glory? Let me point to four things we strive to achieve, though we acknowledge that these are secondary to the task of responding with awe and reverence before a holy and glorious God.

> "It was he who gave some to be . . . pastors and teachers, to prepare God's people for works of service, so that the body of Christ may be built up until we all reach unity in the faith and in the knowledge of the Son of God and become mature."
>
> —Ephesians 4:11–13

1. *We teach others the truth about God.*

   Many people expect worship to be a teaching time. They desire to learn more of eternal truth, to gain more knowledge, to feed their cognitive appetite. And so they primarily focus on the sermon. A preacher approaches sermon-writing in that way, asking, what truth can I convey to worshipers this week?

   Such a function has often been necessary in the life of the church. Early converts possessed only minimal knowledge of the truth. None possessed their own Bibles. In many centuries worshipers were confronted with false teachings and were confused about all the different voices heard in their cities. So worshipers came with an appetite to learn how to discern between truth and error. And they desired to catch a clearer glimpse of God's grand plan for the redemption of all things. Paul reinforced the importance of knowing truth to the Ephesian elders as he bid them farewell: "Now I commit you to God, and to the word of his grace, which can build you up" (Acts 20:31). Consequently for many centuries churches in some traditions were known as preaching centers, and a pulpit was always rather prominent. And when you ask those folks why they came to church they will say, "We came to learn the truth about God."

2. *We aim to experience fellowship.*

Believers *congregate* to worship. They come together and form a body. While a personal and private quiet time has been a part of the Christian lifestyle for many, corporate worship has been even more important. Many worshipers think of their church as a family. They look at each other as brothers and sisters, and they believe they possess a deep spiritual oneness with each other. They sing together, confess their sins together, pray together, and make their professions of faith together. A large part of worship for them is the interaction they have with others. They greet and converse with each other, catch up on the news of each other, and learn of each other's needs, and when they leave they talk about how nice it was to see each other again. Though they may be lonely at times during the week, they are refreshed when they experience their friendship bonds at a time of worship. Christians regarded one another that way right from the beginning of the church. In Acts 2 Luke wrote, "Every day they continued to meet together in the Temple courts. They broke bread in their homes and ate together with glad and sincere hearts, praising God and enjoying the favor all the people" (v. 46). And if you asked them why they came to church, they would say, "We came to be with all our friends again."

3. *In worship we expect to be transformed.*

Nothing seems more logical than this: when we've spent time engaged with the three persons of the Trinity, we can expect to be changed! Could we ever be the same after that? One of the important aims of worship is to make us newer, stronger, and more mature. One person may come to faith in worship, and another may find her faith renewed again. One may confess his sins for the first time and find the freedom of pardon, though another may refuse to confess. One leaves with a greater willingness to obey God, another with a commitment to love others more, still another with a commitment to identify and develop her spiritual gifts, and still others with a deeper resolve to be better parents. One goes away more able to trust God in tough times, and another is more resolved to share her faith with a neighbor and extend practical actions of caring for them. One of the exciting things about leading worship is possessing the confidence that the Holy Spirit will use this time "to prepare God's people for works of service so that the body of Christ may be built up" (Eph 4:12). So if you ask these folks why they came to church they will likely say, "We came to grow in faith."

4. *In worship we expect to be cared for and healed.*

This purpose of worship is the one that seems to be most often neglected and overlooked. We've spoken already about the fact that all worshipers come with needs, because they participate in one way or another in the brokenness of this fallen world. Those needs take a wide variety of forms, and not all are immediately recognizable. (See chapters 1 and 2.) Usually when pastoral care is mentioned, people expect that this is something done in a pastoral counseling session or through a pastoral visit. But our aim is to increase our awareness that important pastoral care can take place during the liturgy, while sitting in the pew. Matthew gave us a glimpse of Christ-likeness that should be present in our worship liturgies. "When (Jesus) . . . saw the crowds, he had compassion on them, because they were harassed and helpless, like sheep without a shepherd." (Matt 9:36)

We will have much more to say in the coming pages about how these purposes might happen or might be improved. But for now, mind you, this is not an endorsement of people who are so concerned about themselves that they want to be cared for "just for the sake of me." This does not mean the purpose of worship is to focus on us. This is not intended to be an encouragement of narcissism. We must remember how often the Bible talks about "growing in the grace and knowledge of our Lord and Savior Jesus Christ" (2 Pet 3:18) and preparing "God's people for works of service" (Eph 4:12), and Paul's address to the Ephesians in which he commends them "to the word of his grace which is able to build you up" (Acts 20:32). God always has his eyes on our wholeness, so we can better serve his purposes. So if you ask these folks why they came to church, they will likely say, "We came because we needed some help and encouragement."

> "But grow in the grace and knowledge of our Lord and Savior Jesus Christ."
>
> —2 Peter 3:18

I hope you always keep that perspective of the worshiping congregation in mind.

TO PONDER AND DISCUSS

1. Which of the five purposes of worship are most commonly upheld by the members of your congregation? Are there others that have not been mentioned?

2. Which of the five purposes of worship listed above are most commonly neglected by your congregation? How could that be improved?

3. Can you recall an instance or two when the final purpose (caring and healing) took place in a recent worship service? What were they?

Chapter 5

Priests and Pastors Who Lead

I F THE ENTIRE LITURGY can be a vehicle for thoughtful pastoral care, *it* certainly puts a large responsibility in the hands of those who serve together as worship planners and leaders, regardless of whether they are clergy or laity. Tasks like these take commitment and giftedness. It will serve us well therefore to turn our attention to the roles of those who lead the liturgy and the qualifications they will need.

When we speak of the work of worship leaders, we are speaking of two quite separate tasks—those who plan the liturgy and those who actually lead it. They may be the same people, or not. In some congregations the ordained pastor might lead large parts of the liturgy; in other congregations laypersons may lead many parts of the liturgy. In either case, ordained or un-ordained, these are key people who should be selected carefully. And once they are selected, a wise church will exercise great care to support and encourage them.

Those who serve as worship leaders should be conscious of the fact that they fill two significant roles. On the one hand they serve in a priestly role. A *priest* is one who stands between God and his people, bringing the two together in a worshipful manner, in the same way that priests in the Old Testament went into the Temple before God on behalf of the worshipers. We are accustomed to thinking of ordained clergy as serving in a priestly role, but today in many churches we also have lay leaders taking on a priestly role. They bring God and his people together in worship. And in addition to the priestly role they take on a *pastoral* role, which involves them in caring for God's children who have come before him in worship. A pastor loves and cares for the children of God in the same way that a shepherd loves and cares for his sheep.

What should those of us who fill these roles be like? What marks should we have in our Christian lives? A congregation will be served well by planners and leaders who exhibit these eight marks.

> "A key factor in whether the liturgy works is the pastor's leadership."
>
> —William Willimon, *Worship as Pastoral Care*, 214.

1. *They maintain a healthy personal worship life.* It almost sounds unnecessary to say that worship leaders need a pattern of worshiping well. Planning and leading worship comes best out of a heart that has been formed by faithful and vital worship practices. And in addition, they now face an additional challenge of worshiping while leading. Many worshipers may not have thought of this, but leaders must put special efforts into their own worship life even while they lead others. They'll have to work hard at balancing the two. It's no small task. The leaders who can both worship and lead simultaneously will be a blessing to all.

2. *They study worship and its issues.* Every congregation today faces a host of questions and issues concerning its worship. We are living in a day of worship renewal in which many questions are being raised, previous practices are being questioned, and efforts at creativity abound. Leaders will provide the best leadership if they have a thoughtful theology of worship and are well aware of the issues of worship in the church. To do that they'll need to read journals, articles, and books and discuss them together. They'll need to attend conferences, workshops, and continuing education events.

They may be part of a peer learning group. They are always learning and growing. Churches that provide resources and funds for these purposes, encourage their worship leaders to participate in conferences for their growth, and provide time for them to do so will serve the congregation well.

3. *They know their fellow worshipers.* They are not strangers to each other. They know the worshipers and much of what they are experiencing. They are aware of the common needs they are likely bringing with them to worship, and also the more unique needs that exist in this particular community and congregation. They read widely about current events. They know the community. They are involved in the life of the congregation. They realize that the most effective worship leaders know their worshipers personally. Those who serve as guest pastors or lead outside of their congregation will have to draw on their general knowledge of human needs and add extra effort to know the community they are entering.

4. *They engage in caring ministries.* Worship leading goes better with a caring spirit. Meeting and getting to know people "behind the scenes" puts them in a position to craft worship that will be sensitive and relevant, and enables them to lead services with empathy and compassion. Those in the choir can serve as a small support group for one another. Those in the praise team can develop great sensitivities to each other's needs.

5. *They pray faithfully.* Of course, the assumption is that all worship leaders will pray for wisdom and discernment as they plan and lead. But they should also have a personal prayer ministry for others. Faithful intercessors make faithful worship leaders. A person who sets aside ample time to intercede for the members of the congregation and community will provide worship that carries an extra level of compassion and understanding. Some worship leaders come to church during the week and pray for those who normally sit in each pew/

chair. Their personal prayer list may include all the members of the choirs, the praise team, or planning committee.

6. *They welcome evaluations.* Many people find evaluations somewhat threatening, yet those evaluations can be the best growth tool for ministry. Mature leaders welcome them when they come from trusted people. Wise is the planning group, praise team, worship committee, or ministry staff that has a high level of trust and honesty together so they can share their evaluative insights. Even simple but honest conversations about what strengths were observed, what weaknesses showed up, and how they might plan or lead a service differently the next time can provide excellent opportunities for growth. The best evaluations will come from carefully selected people who are known for their commitment, maturity, and thoughtfulness.

7. *They communicate openly with others.* Worship committees, a ministry staff, and praise teams that trust each other enough to be candid and honest will serve the church better. They will best achieve such a relationship, however, when they spend time together for something besides their work. Let them be friends who care for each other and enjoy spending some casual time together. Include spouses and families in casual get-togethers.

8. *They pay attention to detail in the worship services.* It's disturbing to discover during a service that something is unclear or proper instructions were not given or details were ignored. Wise leaders will generally walk through the entire service before it begins. All transitions, for instance, should be thought through. When I was in the pastorate, our last task on Saturday noon, before the office was closed for the day, was a walk-through together of the services, so no surprises would show up on Sunday. If your church is charismatic in style and expects/values interruptions in worship, you may want to identify the locations in the liturgy where the interruptions are most likely to appear.

All of us as worship leaders, both those who plan and those who publicly lead, are key people in the worship life of a congregation. We are the priests and pastors to the worshiping congregation. Wise is the church that cares for them well, and encourages them in their ministries.

TO PONDER AND DISCUSS

1. Have you clearly identified the worship leaders in your congregation? Who is responsible for planning your worship? Who are the public liturgists? What do you notice that indicates they understand how important their role is?

2. Carefully review the eight guidelines given above, and then identify

   • Which of these do you most carefully practice?

   • Which of these should receive better attention?

   • What can you do to improve the care of your worship leaders?

3. What kind of arrangements and resources does your congregation have to provide supervision of your worship leaders?

   • Who appoints the leaders?

   • Who is able to give them encouragement in their task?

   • If correction is needed, is it clear who would provide it?

   • Do you have channels in place for thoughtful evaluations?

4. Are you willing to provide training where necessary?

PART TWO

Where Caring Happens Weekly

SECTION TWO LOOKS AT the key elements in a liturgy that offer the greatest potential for caring and healing. Because some churches often design their own liturgy and often are quite different from another, these chapters do not prescribe what to include in the liturgy. They rather examine the most common types of activities in most weekly worship liturgies and how they can be planned and lead in such a way that will offer a ministry of nurture and healing for the worshipers present.

Most weekly liturgies will include, in one form or another, most of these elements, although they may be called by different names. Therefore, your worshiping group will benefit from examining these and comparing the ideas here with your current practice.

Chapter 6

Welcomed by God

SOME OF THE BEST pastoral care can happen at the beginning of the liturgy.

A friend of mine talks about how he felt the first time he went back to church after an absence of some thirty-five years. He felt uncertain and anxious. Sometimes even regular attenders have some of the same concerns and come with hesitancy. Perhaps they've had a bad morning with a family fight at the breakfast table or experienced some failures during the week that make them feel unfit for a holy place. Perhaps another comes with the mental picture of a stern God who is eager to point his judging finger at anyone who steps the least bit out of line. Or maybe she's thinking it's been too long since she's been in church. It's fair to assume that many people come to worship with some form of the question, "Do I really belong here?"

Given this question, worship leaders should keep in mind that entering a church sanctuary can be an anxiety-producing experience. After all, it's not like the mall, where anybody seems to fit, or like a classroom where you've been assigned and are expected, or a coffee shop with a group of friends who are waiting for you. A sanctuary is a different place, a sacred place, and that can be intimidating to many. A sanctuary speaks of the presence of God. It aims to create a sense of awe at encountering a God who listens, cares, hears, and answers, even when we have wounded him by our rejection and disobedience. This astonishment in itself can be nurturing and healing.

So entering church is a major transitional moment that will shape the comfort-level and openness of a worshiper. How well that transition goes may determine whether the worshiper, even a long-time member, comes back.

If we keep these factors in mind we will easily see that our entrance and the first few minutes are an important time when deep caring is needed. The caring that happens in those early moments ideally communicates three messages:

> God invites us into his healing presence with these words:
>
> "I am the Lord, who heals you."
> **Diseased, depressed, dysfunctional, defeated, we come hungering for health that only God can provide.**
> God calls us to bring open eyes, hearing ears, and tender hearts turned toward him, the Great Physician.
> **We bow before him in faith and expectancy!**
>
> —*The Worship Sourcebook,* 54.

1. The people here welcome and accept me. I am not an intruder, and this is not dangerous territory.

2. God welcomes and accepts me. This is his place, and though this is a holy place, unholy people like me are welcomed here.

3. Therefore, it's OK that I am here! I do not need to be afraid or anxious.

To convey these messages, those opening minutes should be planned and led with sensitivity. Consider these dimensions.

Entrance Hospitality

Acts of hospitality that occur during the first few minutes of entering the building are important. Is someone there to greet them? Do they make eye contact? Do they ask their name? Do they notice whether they have children and might like to know if there is a nursery (and where it is)? Do they help find a place to hang their coats? Formally assigning greeters to meet people at the door is a good first step, but only the first step. Better yet is training these greeters to readily engage worshipers in friendly and affirming conversation. All these actions require two things—words and eye-contact. It is healthy for occasional encouragement to be given to all worshipers to express such hospitality to others as they enter. But other matters are also important, such as adequate lighting, a well-stocked and staffed information table, disability access, and hearing assistance are vital too.

Caring Ushers

Few people realize how important good ushers are. And few ushers really grasp the strategic importance of their role. They must be ready to do more than get people to a seat. Ushers need to see themselves as ambassadors for the church, whether the worshipers are guests or long-time attendees. Their warmth of conversation, eagerness to help, and sensitivity to any personal concerns will show care!

Words of Welcome

Somewhere near the beginning, a person must verbalize the fact that all worshipers are welcome. These words may be spoken by the pastor or lay worship leader, but it must be clear they are spoken on behalf of the entire congregation and of God.

Sensitive Prayer

Many churches begin with an opening prayer. Such a prayer ought not to be a formality but an opportunity to make clear that we all come before God with various needs, and we ask God to come and meet us with his grace and mercy.

God's Greeting

While it is important to hear words of welcome from an usher and a worship leader, nothing compares with hearing a welcome directly from God. So throughout history Christian worship has usually included an opening greeting from God. Patterned after the way Paul opened most of his epistles, the pastor raises one or both hands and pronounces welcoming words, such as, "Grace, mercy, and peace to you in the name of the Father, the Son, and the Holy Spirit." It's not just a vague hope, but an actual welcome from the triune God who accepts us into his presence. We need that!

Greeting Each Other

Following God's Greeting, in many churches folks will extend to each other a personal greeting as common as "Good Morning"— a good step in itself. We will discuss later the fact that there are multiple points in the service where this might occur. Historically the church has engaged in "passing the peace" to one another with the words "The peace of Christ to you" or "The Lord be with you" and the response "And also with you." If I've come to worship as a needy person, somewhat unsure of the appropriateness of my presence here, words like these can speak to my heart in a deeply caring way. While some worshipers will find this awkward, occasional explanations of what it means will gradually make it more meaningful.

So the opening ten minutes of a worship time have a large task—one of caring for me in such a way that though I may have come with some reluctance, confusion, or anxiety, I can now say to myself, "It's OK to be here; I am welcomed by others and God, and I can expect to be blessed."

TO PONDER AND DISCUSS

1. Examine the type of relationships demonstrated in your church lobby or narthex before worship. How warm is the

welcome given to those who may be coming as a stranger, or to someone coming with confusion and anxiety? How could it be improved? How much encouragement is given to your congregation to be hospitable?

2. Evaluate the opening moments of your worship service. What happens and what is said that will achieve the goal of leading a worshiper to say, "It's OK to be here, and I can expect to be blessed"?

3. Does your worship service include a greeting from God and the Passing of the Peace? If so, is it done meaningfully? If not, is some instruction and explanation needed?

Welcome to the worship of the Lord today.
We come with all our needs and concerns.
Some of us have been so blessed and we are grateful;
some of us are discouraged and we need new hope;
some of us have experienced God's care in deep ways this week;
some of us wonder whether he has forgotten us;
some of us have deep and abiding assurance;
and some of us carry a load of regrets.
Whatever our circumstance and whatever our needs,
come today, let him embrace you with his love and care.

—A Pastor

Chapter 7

Sitting Together

W HERE WE SIT, AND the fact that we sit together for the liturgy, has significance. It may seem beyond the scope of our
concern here, but if we take a careful look at it, I think we'll see
how important it is. While it is something that worship leaders
cannot direct, it nonetheless reveals how entrenched habits can be
either opportunities or obstacles.

My family always sat in about the same place in worship. It
was "our pew," though nobody ever quite dared say that. Now that
I'm sitting in a pew again on most Sundays, I find we sit in about
the same place again. As a matter of fact, I notice that most people
do.

But sometimes I wonder if there is a caring issue associated
with where and how people sit in church. Does where they sit, and
how they behave there, speak about how much they care, or don't
care, for others?

A congregation is just that—a group of people congregating
together. A church is a group of called-out people who belong to
each other. They call each other brother and sister. The assumption
is that a bond exists and that relationships matter. Should that affect where worshipers sit?

So let's take a look at our practices of sitting together—where
and how we do it. It might bring to mind some factors we ought

to consider. Five questions can be raised to help us dig into this review. *Is it wise to sit in the same area regularly?*

I already cited the fact that most of us do sit in the same place week after week. We usually explain that we just are creatures of habit. Patterns help us to experience security and safety. Though this may explain the practice, it doesn't go far in evaluating it. A habit may be good one or a poor one. On the one hand I find it's a good thing to sit in the same place, particularly in a larger church, because when I sit in the same general area, as others do, then I can become acquainted with those who are near me. Seeing them week after week aids in building a relationship with this smaller group. Otherwise, I'm sitting with strangers every week and am never able to build much of a relationship with them. However, it might be advantageous to move around each week and broaden the circle of acquaintances. The choice highlights the fact that one of the criteria we might use to decide where we sit is to ask, how can I best build relationships with these other people who are my brothers and sisters?

Shall I Sit on the Fringe?

Some sanctuaries are built with some convenient fringe areas. It may be the back row, or a section off on the side, or a balcony area. These areas are somewhat removed from others and provide for some privacy, aloneness, and an easy exit. I understand that some folks may have other good reasons for preferring these places, especially if they are somewhat introverted and the sanctuary is not full, but there is always the possibility that fringe places are chosen to avoid interaction with other worshipers. In one of my congregations, two people always arrived at least forty-five minutes before the worship service began, always took their customary place in the back row, and at the end of the service left the building and were in their car before others could exit the building. For whatever reason (and there were some) they selected their seats to avoid relationships. Where we sit will indeed impact how much caring we receive and give in a time of worship.

Where in the Row Should I Sit?

Perhaps this doesn't seem like a significant issue, but if we carefully examine what happens as people take their seats, it takes on greater significance. I understand that some need to sit on the end of the row because they have a special role in the service and need to get out. But consider these possibilities as well. When I enter the row and immediately sit on the end, I might be sending a message that suggests I really hope that no one else comes in this row with me, whereas if I move to the center of the row, I make it clear that I hope someone comes to join me. If I sit on the end of the row and require that others crawl past me to enter the pew, I am saying that my preference is more important than your convenience. Where we sit can easily speak of "me first" gestures.

How Much Shall I Interact with Neighbors in the Row?

Interaction is a big consideration. Some traditions encourage a time of quiet before worship so that a time of personal preparation for worship can take place. Some churches will even ask worshipers to keep silence before the service, so others have a quiet time to pray and enjoy the peace of the sanctuary. This will, of course, minimize interaction. But many more congregations today encourage conversation before the service begins. I have been in some worship services in which those who sat next to me never even acknowledged I was there, and their silence felt like rejection. In others, a greeting was exchanged with perhaps some minor conversation, which is better and may

> Our pastor has an excellent relationship with the children of the congregation, so when he invites them to come forward for a Children's Message, they come eagerly. One Sunday, while the children were coming forward, the pastor's smile grew wider and wider, until he said, "you know, you are just like all those older folks out there. You hurry into church just so you can get your favorite seat!" A giggle rippled throughout the sanctuary.
>
> —Howard Vanderwell

pave the way for better conversations after the service. Others have used that time to get acquainted and express a welcome.

Two other opportunities for interaction exist. When the peace of Christ is passed, it can be done in a warm and genuine manner. And when worshipers near us have any difficulty finding worship materials, locating the page numbers of readings, determining what comes next, we can give assistance to them. In addition, be sure to introduce yourself at the close of the service and do not let them leave without a welcome.

Do My Actions Communicate Acceptance?

This, of course, is the bottom line. Consider it an act of the providence of God that you happen to be sitting together in church, and God has placed you together there because he intends that something will occur between you that will communicate acceptance, caring, and service. Just imagine that the person or family next to you is a guest or a newcomer who comes with anxiety and uncertainty, wondering if she or he will be accepted. Imagine that they carry some personal burden with them today and are hoping for some indication that God and this church cares about them. This acceptance can take many different forms, but it will never happen when people ignore each other.

TO PONDER AND DISCUSS

1. Why do you suppose that so many people sit in nearly the same area in church each week? Can you think of other reasons than those cited here? How can we make the most of that practice?

2. Is it legitimate to expect that people who sit near each other in church should view it as an opportunity to care for and support one another in some way? How could that happen?

3. Of the five questions asked in this chapter, which two do you think are most strategic for your congregation?

Chapter 8

Liturgy with Room for All

My mother taught me a lot about what the church should be like. She was a genuine Christian woman who wanted nothing more than a life of vital and biblical worship and children who loved the Lord. But she experienced great challenges nearly all of her adult life, because she had advanced rheumatoid arthritis. Every day she lived with pain and limited mobility. Walkers and wheelchairs were always fixtures around our home. Surgeries were regular occurrences. It was always assumed that the rest of us would make allowance in our schedules to "help mom" and would not complain. My father set the tone for that. I watched my parents deal with constant obstacles, and I learned a lot about them and about what the Christian church should be like.

Congregations need to be sensitive to the reality that many people have some kind of disability. Disabilities are so varied that we might think of basic categories, such as physical disabilities (involving issues of mobility, strength, and function), sensory disabilities (involving hearing and vision), emotional and mental health (involving the ability to respond and relate to others), and intellectual disabilities. Churches often find it easy to overlook such needs and therein lies a special challenge for the church at worship to practice caring.

Dan Vander Plaats, an educator, has helpfully outlined five stages on the journey of becoming more caring.[1] I strongly suggest that as a worship leader you be aware of these.

- *Stage 1—Ignorance:* I do not know such people, I have no interest in getting to know them, and God probably can't use people who are so broken.

- *Stage 2—Pity:* I feel sorry for those people, and I feel so blessed by God that people like me are able to help them.

- *Stage 3—Care:* Like me, people with disabilities were created in God's image, and someone must take the time to care for them, help them, and greet them.

- *Stage 4—Friendship:* God has brought different people into my church, I have gotten to know them, and my life is better for having known them. We all benefit as we grow in friendship together.

- *Stage 5—Co-Laborers:* God has called each of us to serve and praise him. The same is true for our brothers and sisters with disabilities. We can all give, and we can all receive.

Becoming a caring church in our worship as well as the rest of our life is not only a matter of learning certain actions, but is rather a journey in attitude toward ourselves and toward other people. As we move through these five stages, we will become more aware of the barriers that we have unintentionally erected, of the way in which we have devalued those who are different from us, and how we can better treat and relate to them.

Beginning this journey will require worship planners and leaders, and hopefully others within the congregation with them, to take several steps. The journey begins with the conviction that people with disabilities are *people* first of all. All people are valuable because we are created in God's image, and neither our

---

1. Vander Plaats, Dan and Elim Christian Services, "The 5 Stages: Changing Attitudes."

abilities nor disabilities can change that. We are different not in our value, but in the ways we are able to serve.

Once we have taken that step, we are in a position to recognize which practices in our worshiping community aid a caring ministry and which interfere with it. We can become more aware of our physical accessibility (how we make it easier or more difficult for some to join us, and what needs to be done to improve that) and our communication accessibility (how we can best provide for those with sensory challenges). We can also think about how our ministries can promote growth and fellowship, and the multiple ways in which people with various disabilities can serve in ministries related to worship, such as reading, singing, prayer, and so forth.

Perhaps a profitable exercise for your church leadership team would be to assess what would happen in worship services if these people came to church on a given Sunday.

> Kelsey and Chris are sister and brother, both with some disabilities. Kelsey obviously has Down's syndrome. Chris's cognitive abilities are limited but his appearance does not show that. However in conversation both become obvious. They were new members at church, so few people knew of their situation.
>
> They were both baptized much earlier and now desired to make their profession of faith and come to the Lords' Table. One Sunday both of them stood before the congregation and were asked several simple questions about their trust in Jesus Christ and their desire to take communion. Kelsey's mannerisms and Chris' halting speech made two things clear: they both had disabilities, and when it came to the Lord's Table, none of that mattered.
>
> —Used with permission

- Chuck uses a wheelchair, and he's a fairly large man. Could he enter the church? The sanctuary? Where can his wheelchair be placed? Could he sit with his friends? Could he use the bathroom?

- Sally has autism, and some behavioral issues appear from time to time. Would she be welcome in the sanctuary with her family? How would others react if there were some disturbance? How would the pastor feel? How would others handle some disturbance?

- Tom has macular degeneration in both eyes and is legally blind. Will he find a place in the worshiping congregation? Will he be welcomed and helped? Will there be some materials to help him follow the worship service?

- Marcy has a limited cognitive ability but loves to come to worship with her family. Will she be able to understand much that is said? Will there be any materials at her level that will help her sing and follow the thoughts in the service? How will others relate to her? Will they mind when she sings differently?

- Marvin was burned seriously in an accident. He has recovered well, but now his face is significantly disfigured by scars. He's quite conscious of others staring at him, but he loves to worship. How would your congregation handle his presence in worship?

Not all image-bearers are alike. But all are valuable, and God wants all to worship him regardless of abilities. Accomplishing this will take a great deal of mature Christ-like caring.

Maybe the best place for the leaders of our congregation to begin is not to ask about the response the congregation might have, but to ask ourselves about our own personal reaction to making room for people with such needs. What is yours?

TO PONDER AND DISCUSS

1. What Scripture passages can you recall that show us how Christ would caringly treat those with developmental and cognitive needs?

2. Can you cite a recent instance in your congregation when someone with disabilities came to worship and your worship pace was not accessible or they were not treated well? What happened and how was it resolved?

3. And can you cite a recent instance when someone with disabilities came to worship and a helpful caring spirit was shown them? How was that demonstrated?

4. Review the five stages that Dan Vander Plaats formulated (see page 47). Which most accurately characterizes you? Your congregation?

Chapter 9

Learning to Use Words That Care

YOU'VE PROBABLY NOTICED IT. Words are everywhere in a worship service. Several thousand words can be spoken or sung during a time of worship. Often we hear the complaint that liturgies are too wordy. But since words are vehicles that convey meaning, the potential for good is high, though they must be chosen carefully.

Some words are part of a standard or historic liturgy, or a song with a text written by a poet. Other words are composed by a preacher and delivered as the sermon. Still other words are printed on a worship sheet to direct the actions of worshipers. But many others are composed by liturgists to be spoken during worship, some carefully planned and some spontaneous. It is true that generally people today depend less on words and more on visuals

> "Worship depends on words. God's revelation to us is given not only in creation but also in words that communicate all we need to know about God, ourselves and our salvation. Our communal worship is made possible because we have words to speak to each other, to call each other to worship, to speak common prayers, and encourage each other in the faith."
>
> —*The Worship Sourcebook*, 21.

and images, yet the sheer number of words in worship still can be overwhelming.

It is worth our while, therefore, to carefully assess the words in worship to determine their accuracy, their level of truthfulness, and their spirit of caring. Three methodologies might help us in this evaluation.

- We can try to listen self-consciously during a worship service to pick up anything that violates the principles of accuracy, truthfulness, and caring. This will require great objectivity and self-awareness.

- We can personally review a worship service by listening to an audio or video recording of the service. Doing this a few days after the service will increase our ability to listen objectively and enable us to recognize factors we might have missed before.

- We can conduct a group review and assessment, probably with other worship planners and leaders. Such a group assessment with specific questions in mind can be helpful and enlightening as we exchange observations.

Six key questions are necessary for this evaluation of our words in worship. Use these often.

1. *Are these words truth?* God, who is the source of all truth, certainly will require truth in all that is said. The words in worship are shaping worshipers and teaching them what to believe. The words that we sing form our convictions of truth more than we realize. The sermon must proclaim God's truth clearly, the songs must express it accurately, and the verbal expressions of worship leaders must always be consistent with what is true. Anything false is unwelcome.

2. *Are they honest?* The words spoken and sung must be an accurate description of what we are feeling right now, of reality, of experience as it is, and not as we wish it were. To tell God we are all delighted and overjoyed to be here in his presence this morning fails to acknowledge that many people may not

feel that way at all and will only be convinced we don't understand their struggles and ambivalence. And sometimes being honest before God may require a candid lament rather than a nice prayer. The psalmists are our models for candid and earthy rather than pious and positive speech. I remember the day our congregation broke new ground in our ability to be honest when an elder was hospitalized with depression, and the family gave permission to announce to the congregation the cause of his hospitalization and not use some euphemism.

3. *Are they empathetic?* Such words are readily recognized as those that promote understanding and compassion. Often they are spoken by someone who has already walked in the sufferers' shoes. Empathetic words carry pain in them, vicarious pain, and they hold out both empathy and a promise of hope and help. They are spoken with a voice, inflection, gestures, and facial expressions that convey care. Caring words do not ignore uncomfortable realities.

4. *Are they welcoming?* How easy it is for our words to communicate that some are accepted and some are not, some belong to "our group" and some don't, that some have all the qualities needed, and others do not. To be sure, such discrimination is seldom done intentionally; it happens without thinking. Our words can express a welcome to all who come in worship, yet at the same time those same words can seem to point to how important it is to be a "regular member," leaving out those who are occasional attendees.

5. *Are they inclusive?* Some congregations are sensitive to inclusivity regarding gender, and to violate it is offensive to the community. But we need the same sensitivity in other areas also. How many times on Mother's Day have mothers been extolled and praised for their beautiful role in molding young children, yet others sitting in the pews are, for example, infertile and hurting deeply because of their inability to bear children and their feeling that others are not sensitive to that. And on Father's Day how many worship leaders have prayed

lavish prayers for the witness of Christian fathers and have ignored the pain and sorrow of others who have been the victims of abusive fathers or live in a home where Father is absent. And how often has marriage been praised, putting couples in the spotlight, while singles and widows sit in forgotten silence. In another place I speak about the inclusiveness that needs to be extended toward those with disabilities of all sorts. Inclusivity needs to be communicated by carefully chosen caring words.

6. *Are they divisive?* If words can heal, they can also divide. If they can reconcile, they can also separate, both intentionally and unintentionally. Words that are kind will avoid this risk of separating people; words that are judgmental will easily cause it. It's easy to speak about "we" and "they," "us" and "them," "our kind" and "their kind." We can too easily point to the differences that separate us and emphasize those differences, putting others down, rather than uphold the similarities that bind us together.

The church is a community of grace. Grace is to be real here, so real that it is obvious in the songs that we sing and the sermons that we hear, but also in the words that we speak to each other.

Blessed and happy is the church that prepares all words carefully and thoughtfully, and hesitates to speak extemporaneously. Wise is the worship leader who refuses to speak off-the-cuff, but insists on taking the time to choose words well.

> "Essentially, worship leaders must mean what they say and must themselves be worshiping while they are leading. They must model authenticity in worship in the sense that they are fully actively, and consciously attentive to what they are doing. Their authenticity naturally invites worshipers to worship authentically themselves."
>
> —Debra and Ron Rienstra, *Worship Words*, 97.

TO PONDER AND DISCUSS

1. Recall and evaluate the words spoken in a recent worship service. Do you feel they were well-chosen and thoughtful? Cite examples of this.

2. Do you and your colleagues have adequate methods in place for regular assessment and review of the words in your worship? If not, how could you begin establishing such a process?

3. Of the six key questions suggested for word review (truth, honesty, caring, welcoming, inclusivity, and divisiveness), which are most frequently violated in your worship services? How can you improve the words you use?

Chapter 10

Receiving God's Pardon

I F YOU WANT TO start an energetic conversation, or even a debate, ask a group of pastors and worship planners what they think about having a ritual for the confession of sin in their worship. You'll likely hear quite a variety of comments, including "We do it every week without fail," "People don't feel guilty today so why have it," "That doesn't speak to me," "What a downer to lay a guilt trip on people," and "it's the best gift we can give them." I'm sure you have heard such comments at one time or another.

Let's acknowledge that our position on this matter will most certainly be shaped by our experiences. I remember the days of my childhood when the time of confession followed the same routine every week. We heard the Ten Commandments, a prayer of confession by the pastor (same words every week, it seemed), and then the assurance of pardon (same verse every week). There seemed to be little investment by anyone, little energy, but we, if we paid attention, were satisfied that we had done our duty. And yet, looking back, I must admit that I can now see how such a regular practice did serve to form my faith.

On the other hand I recall a jarring conversation with one of my parishioners who had recently joined our congregation after growing up in the Roman Catholic Church. We were talking about the adjustment she experienced, and I quizzed her about which of the adjustments was the most difficult. She didn't hesitate in her response at all. "I'm usually frustrated when you lead us in the service of confession." I was taken aback, but when I talked with her further I was even more surprised at her response. "You pastors frustrate me," she bluntly said. "You have us make confession and then you speak in vague terms that never seem to get to the point about whether I'm forgiven or not. It's like you don't feel free to come right out and tell me, 'God has forgiven you.' Don't just beat around the bush; tell me straight . . . am I forgiven? I need to hear it!" Now I know she was accustomed to a priest who claimed the authority to absolve people of their sins, and I didn't believe I should do that, but she had a personal need to hear the word from the Lord that for the sake of Christ she could be sure her sins were forgiven. She needed me to say to her, "On the basis of Christ's finished work and his sure promises, your sins are forgiven!"

The conversation led me to wonder why pastors and worship leaders today are so hesitant to include the confession of sin within worship. Is it because we are hesitant to speak God's word of assurance? Do we really believe people have no need for pardon? Do we think they'll resist a church that tells them they ought to confess? Or are we not sensitive to the fact that one of the personal needs we all bring to worship is the need for cleansing—and that pardon is the very heart of the Christian gospel? Or have we perhaps become satisfied with a bland spirituality?

I like the way Neal Plantinga, Jr., President Emeritus of Calvin Theological Seminary, expressed the need for confession and assurance in his devotional book *Beyond Doubt*.[1] Confessing our sins, he said, is like taking out the garbage. He called it an extremely healthy thing

> "Sometimes you pastors frustrate me. You have us make confession, and then you speak in vague terms about whether we are forgiven or not. It's like you don't feel free to come right out and tell me, 'God has forgiven you.' Don't just beat around the bush; tell me straight that I'm forgiven. I need to hear it!"
>
> —A Parishioner to her pastor

1 Plantinga, *Beyond Doubt*, 54.

to do. We may live in a nice clean house, but we still need those regular trips to take out the garbage. And if we don't, it soon will pile up and "nice and clean" will no longer apply to our house!

People today may like to claim that they don't experience guilt, but we should remember that the real presence of guilt is not dependent on whether we *feel* the guilt or not. We can *be* guilty without any conscious awareness of it. Though we may call such guilt other names, the fact of the matter is that we humans have a frequently strained relationship with God because we have not obeyed him as we should. He knows that, and we do too, but often we don't want to acknowledge it. So when we are in the presence of God we need to be led in certain regular disciplines that aim for our peace, though we might not desire to do it. Our faith is formed through such actions.

Marva Dawn once wrote, "The explicit announcement that all my sins, known and unknown, have been pardoned through Jesus Christ is the best good news available anywhere in the world. Why on earth would our churches not want to speak these glad tidings to guilty and burdened hearts?"[2] So I'll argue for the regular inclusion of a time of confession in our liturgies. But while I do, I'll also argue for leaders who are both careful and creative in the way in which they plan and lead this critical part of the worship service. The actions of confession will best serve the worshipers when four marks characterize it:

1. *Fresh and creative planning efforts.* Wise are the planners and leaders who craft these few moments of the service creatively and lovingly. We must guard against routine words mouthed as dull habit. We find that our faith is formed through the repetition of disciplines that are done meaningfully.

2. *A warm and caring spirit.* This is not the time for any expression of rejection or judgment by either the church or God. Most sinners know about that internally, and that's exactly why they desire to be cleansed. So let us exude the spirit of Christ who said, "Come to me, all who are weary

---

2. Dawn, *How Shall We Worship?* 130–31.

and burdened, and I will give you rest" (Matt 11:28). This is the optimum moment to portray exactly what the gospel is all about.

3. *Clear words of pardon.* Those of us who are Protestants are sometimes not comfortable saying "I absolve you," but we certainly can speak words that clearly affirm, "In the name of Christ, who gave himself on the cross, you are forgiven just as surely as you have confessed. So go in peace." This is not the time for an oblique passage, but for a direct statement for the heart of the contrite. Say it clearly, lovingly, and with eye contact.

4. *A joyful response.* Worshipers should then have opportunity to respond to such pardon with a heart-felt expression of thanksgiving. It may be a song of thanks and praise, or an exclamation such as, "Thanks be to God," or it may include the testimony of one who has been forgiven, or the communal act of passing the peace with words such as, "The peace of the Lord be with you, too." Some use the offering as a tangible expression of response. The mouth and the heart need to express the joy that accompanies the "rest" of being pardoned. And God is glorified by hearing it!

Confessing sins and receiving God's pardon are rich elements of a Christian's worship. Those who lead worship may rightly feel privileged to lead God's people in this part of their encounter.

TO PONDER AND DISCUSS

1. Does the tradition of your congregation and its worship include a service of confession? How have you been blessed by it?

2. Describe a recent time of confession that communicated special caring to you. What made it that way?

3. Evaluate the analogy that making confession of our sins is like taking out the garbage. Do you agree that it is a good

illustration to use? Why or why not? What are the consequences for neglecting it?

> "While it is true that we have sinned,
> it is a greater truth that we are forgiven
> through God's love in Jesus Christ.
> To all who humbly seek the mercy of God I say,
> in Jesus Christ your sin is forgiven."
> **Thanks be to God.**
> — *The Worship Sourcebook,* 121.

Chapter 11

Passing the Peace

PASSING THE PEACE HAS a long history in the worship of many Christian churches. However, it takes many forms and is treated in widely different ways. To some it seems as though it's an empty ritual, to others it is anticipated with eagerness. In some churches it may take the form of the standard opening statement: "The Lord be with you; *and also with you.*" Another church can't get past the habitual "Good Morning!" assuming such a greeting somehow qualifies as passing the peace. In another they may routinely shake hands and say, "Peace." But in another it takes a big block of time while worshipers greet each other with warm and caring hugs, even scurrying to the other side of the room to meet someone with an embrace. Still others exclude any such expression altogether. At times the distinction between a greeting and passing the peace is not clear in their minds and confusion results.

This could be a gift we rarely open fully. These words could possess a gesture of care that has been too often ignored. Fundamental to Christian worship is the conviction that we gather as those who know Christ's reconciling love and believe that, because of the forgiveness of our sins, we are reconciled to Christ and therefore the possibility of genuine fellowship with each other exists among us. This reconciliation needs tangible expression. The passing of the peace is a gesture that expresses and proclaims this reconciliation and peace with one another. Rich is the church whose members can step past their self-consciousness and meaningfully engage in the passing of the peace.

Some of the difficulty, of course, lies in the fact that in most of our churches we sit in straight rows, all facing forward. Our architecture has been shaped by our need to see and hear the one who is preaching. But when we sit in straight rows to face the preacher, we see the back of most people's heads and perhaps a side view of a few others. Rarely do forgiven and reconciled people face each other and practice their relationship in Christ. Such a seating arrangement makes passing the peace a difficult task. It will take deliberate effort for worship leaders to teach and encourage this practice to such a congregation.

> Since God has forgiven us in Christ, let us forgive one another.
> The peace of our Lord Jesus Christ be with you all.
> **And also with you.**
>
> —*The Worship Sourcebook*, 125.

Maybe we ought to clarify why there should be such an act in the liturgy and how it developed. Underlying this act is the fact that as worshipers we are brothers and sisters together, reconciled members of a community founded on God's unconditional acceptance and forgiveness. This is the kingdom of grace that brings peace. And so this act of passing the peace is a gesture expressing who we are and what we are meant to be for each other. It's a pledge that we intend to keep faith with one another, to accept one another, to care and pray for each other. In God's greeting to us we are assured he welcomes us into his presence, and now with this act we assure each other of our welcome for them.

As we noted above, two perspectives compete for attention—that this is a social greeting and that it is the actual passing the peace of Christ. Where it is located in the worship service will tilt our thinking toward one perspective or the other. If you find it near the opening of the service, it will have social greeting overtones. If it is located after the assurance of pardon, or perhaps within the liturgy of the Lords Supper, it more clearly becomes an expression of the fact that as we have been forgiven, we experience unity with each other.

Imagine these scenarios. Mark enters the worship service as a stranger, with all the uncertainties that first-time visitors feel. When the peace is passed to him he still experiences some awkwardness and doesn't know quite what to do. But as it proceeds he feels less like an uncertain stranger and more like a welcomed brother. Gracie is an eight-year-old who often feels overlooked in church because she's not an adult, but today an adult turns toward her and wishes her the peace of Christ. She's thrilled. Stan is a teenager who has some personal struggles, but when other adults give the peace of Christ to him his self-esteem is strengthened. Mary and Sue have had some harsh words with each other recently because they disagreed on a matter under consideration in the church. But after they extend the peace of Christ to each other, they both find it harder to nurse the grudge they've been holding. Healthy is the church at worship that pays attention to passing the peace as a proclamation of the gospel and an act of Christian togetherness, and not merely as a social ritual.

You will find that such an act takes on significance and meaning when you observe these guidelines.

- *Make it spiritual, rather than social.* There is a big difference between turning to someone and saying, "The peace of Christ be with you" and greeting someone with "Good morning." It's a polite social custom to greet others with "good morning," but please understand this is a primarily social greeting, generally empty of any spiritual significance. In a time of worship we look for events and words that carry worshipers beyond social custom. It is helpful to include in the worship sheet the title "passing (or sharing) the peace of Christ," rather than "greeting each other."

- *Make eye contact when you pass the peace.* Personal communication with eye contact takes place on a deeper level than when there is no eye contact. Let your eyes meet and communicate the peace that the words signify.

- *Say it with warmth of voice.* Surely you have experienced how one person's tone of voice communicates far more than words alone. Special deep words like "the peace of Christ" should never be spoken with a drab, monotone voice. No mumbling here; say these words with warmth and caring.

- *Touch when you greet.* A greeting spoken, even with a warm voice and eye contact, is missing something without physical contact. The culture of your community will likely shape how this touch will be expressed. At the least it should be a handshake. Better yet is the two-hand shake. But perhaps your community communicates warmth and acceptance best with a hug.

Blessed is the church that discovers the richness and beauty of passing the peace, and rich are the members who share with each other this gesture that signals clearly that we are reconciled to God and therefore to one another.

> In his abundant grace, God has forgiven us.
> God has freed us from our sin
> and transformed our grief into joy.
> Now we can be at peace with God.
> In gratitude for that great gift,
> let us share God's peace with one another.
> —*The Worship Sourcebook*, 125.

TO PONDER AND DISCUSS

1. What does your congregation's practice of "passing of the peace" communicate about your congregation's identity? How comfortable are your members in doing so?

2. Does your congregation have an understanding of the deeper and broader meaning of the act of passing the peace? If they

see it as merely another social greeting, what is needed to help worshipers' understand it as a spiritual gift?

3. Where is the passing of the peace normally found in your order of service? Is that the best place? Would another location in the liturgy make it more meaningful? Where might that be and how would you explain that to the congregation?

Chapter 12

When We Sing

I'M SURE YOU HAVE experienced how thrilling rich and hearty congregational singing can be. Sometimes I think God's Spirit often fills us the most during such singing. But not all singing is like that. While I've found God's healing spirit poured out during singing, I've also seen other folks bored during times of singing. And I've also seen how music and song can become a viciously divisive influence. Songs can unite us, and they can divide us. They can heal, and they can hurt.

The church is one of the last places in society where people sing together, where they—no matter how many people and how different they are—become "one voice." The church has a long history of joining in celebrative song. Nehemiah's choirs sang together so vigorously that their "rejoicing . . . could be heard far away" (Neh 12:43).

> "When the church gathers in worship, earth and heaven converge. When we sing we are not singing by ourselves. There is a higher song going on above ours and a deeper song going on beneath ours."
>
> —Reggie Kidd, *With One Voice: Discovering Christ's Song in Our Worship*, 115.

Songs, properly and sincerely sung, give praise and honor to God. So we sing *for him*. And at times we may sing *for others*, encouraging and inspiring them by our praise and our testimonies. But it's also true that we sing *for ourselves,* giving expression to our thoughts and feelings. All three of these warrant more careful examination. Hurting worshipers who have come with all manner of needs can be helped and healed by song. Let me suggest some ways in which that happens. Recall which of these you have experienced. Perhaps you can add others.

1. *When we sing, we experience unity.* I may be twelve years old and you might be eighty-six, but we become one voice. I'm male and you are female, but our voices blend. You are trained to sing well, and I'm not, but we can both participate. You are a mature believer, and I'm struggling hard, but we sing together.

2. *When we sing we create beauty.* Hearing the whole congregation sing is a wondrous sound. A small sound becomes a large sound; a single note becomes a complex of sound waves. Young join old; sopranos join basses, and they both join altos and tenors. We call that *harmony.* And harmony with all its healing power is a beautiful sound in a world with so much dissonance! In all our singing, strength and beauty come through. The sound of song can easily overrule the ugliness of our world.

3. *When we sing we exhibit equality.* Everyone is welcome—no age barriers, no auditions required, no ranking. My father now sings in glory, but here on earth he sang with a monotone voice. The only thing he knew is that when those little black circles on the page climbed the staff, he went louder. But he always felt free to sing as heartily as anyone else, and he did. One author said we have a problem with the "American Idol Syndrome" in our churches, wanting to honor most those who can sing best. People too quickly feel second rate if they don't make a golden sound. Too bad!

4. *When we sing we stir up our belief.* I think often of the father who brought his son to Jesus to be healed. When Jesus asked, "Do you believe?" he candidly admitted, "I do believe; help me overcome my unbelief." Most of us experience that from

time to time. Singing songs of faith is one of the best ways to stir up our belief and make some progress in overcoming our unbelief. The more I sing "In Christ alone," the more strongly I stand with him. The more I sing "Amazing grace, how sweet the sound," the more I marvel at his grace in my life. Our voice directs our heart to what it should embrace.

5. *When we sing we address God with our thoughts.* It's so healthy for God's children to address him, but we must admit we do it too seldom. Even our prayer life gets shallow and stale, and we fail to directly tell God just how much we love him. And that's not good for our hearts. But in singing together "Father, we love you" and "In my life, Lord, be glorified" my heart is relieved to be finally saying directly to him what I have really wanted to say all along. In my song, I affirm the grand theme that a righteous God is on the throne.

6. *When we sing we can express our pain.* Sure, there is a lot of pain in life, and when they are heavy our hearts need to express it. The pews on Sunday morning have more pain cumulatively than most of us care to imagine. But so much of it is silent, buried, private. That isn't always healthy. So it's a big step to begin easing that pain by naming it and expressing it to God. Not all songs can be praise and thanks. Together we also sing, "Jesus, draw me nearer as I labor through the storm; you have called me to this passage and I'll follow though I'm worn." God welcomes our honesty with him.

7. *When we sing we can pray for others.* We call that vicarious singing. Others, near and far, just might be hurting so much they can't even sing their own prayers. So we do it for them. I can sing "Precious Lord, take my hand, lead me on, help me stand; I am tired, I am weak, I am worn." And I can sing it with tears rolling down my cheeks while I am healthy and well, for though I may be in a healthy spot, I sing this prayer for our family members or the sufferers of this world who cannot sing it themselves.

8. *When we sing we can catch the big picture of the global church.* Too often we feel lonely, as though our church is the only one around. But that scene changes in worship when global songs are included. When I sing something from the Hispanic church, or an African American Spiritual, or from Asia, I am encouraged to remember that this holy apostolic church of which I am a part is a worldwide church. I am lifted beyond national and cultural boundaries to see the one, worldwide church united in Christ.

Congregational singing can be a healing time for those who come to worship with all their needs. In your worship work be sure you pay close attention to it.

> "Think of singing as a language that allows us to embody our love for our Creator. Song is a means he has given us to communicate our deepest affections, to have our thoughts exquisitely shaped, and to have our spirits braced for the boldest of obediences. Through music, God draws us deeper into a love affair with himself."
>
> —Reggie Kidd, *With One Voice: Discovering Christ's Song in our Worship*, 14.

TO PONDER AND DISCUSS

1. How would you rate the singing of your congregation? Which of the marks mentioned here show up best? Which are absent?

2. Identify several factors in your congregation that aid good, healthy singing. How can they be affirmed and encouraged?

3. Identify factors that may stand in the way of good congregational singing at your church? What could be done to overcome them?

Chapter 13

When We Pray

Prayers offered during worship can be such an anomaly—a sacred time when humans can actually communicate with God, and yet a time when they experience boredom and distraction. When the worship leader announces, "Let us pray," some lift their hearts in expectation and astonishment that God listens to us, while others slouch down in the pew and prepare to disengage. Wise is the worship leader who is aware of both the opportunities and dangers of leading the worshiping congregation in prayer.

Worship leaders need to be conscious of the phenomenal privilege they have of serving as priest and actually leading people into the presence of Almighty God for a conversation! We worship a God who listens and responds! While talking to God may seem intimidating, we ought to sense the profound privilege of such a practice. Wise is the worship leader who communicates such an attitude to the worshipers. Nowhere does a worship leader step into the role of priest more obviously than when becoming the voice of the people before God!

We must assume that worshipers bring their own struggles with prayer into worship, so leading this element of worship will not be so easy. Some of them may have given up on prayer, finding praying just too hard. Some may have become discouraged, because no matter how hard they try, their mind will not stay focused. And still others may feel that so many important prayers of theirs have not made any difference and there just is no use praying anymore.

Blessed is the congregation who has a pastor and worship leaders who (1) are sensitive to these struggles, (2) have developed a rich personal practice of prayer, and (3) are eager to help form worshipers into more earnest pray-ers.

> "In the event that you feel the need for personal prayer for yourself or someone else, Prayer Servants will be waiting for you in the narthex at the close of this service."
>
> —A Worship Leader

So how can you become a leader who will say "Let us pray" and expect worshipers to welcome the invitation?

1. *Be sure you know the needs of others.* The most able prayer leader is the one who is deeply involved in caring for others. They are people who know others, who struggle with them, who listen to their questions and doubts, and take time to be with them. The prayer leader knows not only the general needs of all people, but also the particular needs of this community and congregation. At times we've handed out cards in the morning service and asked the worshipers to jot down whatever they'd like us to pray for at the evening service. Some churches will have a "prayer requests" box in the narthex, and worship leaders check it before each worship service. Some congregations encourage worshipers to offer prayer requests (both praise and petition) in the service—a practice that works best in a smaller group, but not so well in a larger group. Among all your efforts as a prayer leader, learning the needs and requests of others is helpful.

2. *Prepare carefully.* When we pray "off the cuff," our words can sound so sincere and personal, but we often come to realize later that there were big holes in the prayer—needs and concerns that we unintentionally missed when we too easily fell back into familiar clichés. Wise is the pastor or worship leader who gives the same careful attention to the ministry of

praying as the ministry of preaching, who prepares the prayer throughout the week. One helpful tool is to keep a "prayer list" on our desk all week long. Every time we encounter another need in our conversations, pastoral work, reading or listening to the news, we jot down another idea. Every nudging of the Spirit during the week is preserved for inclusion in the prayer on Sunday. Careful preparation will give us time and attention to craft clear words and will more readily carry worshipers along with us. Most worship leaders consider five to seven minutes sufficient for such a prayer, but the culture of your congregation will usually determine the length of the prayers.

3. *Pray thanks and praise.* Many of the worshipers in the service have reasons to give God thanks. They'd like to praise God for who he is, but they can't really find the words to do so to their satisfaction. When we lead in prayer, we become their mouths. We find words for them to express what's in their hearts and thoughts they haven't been able to verbalize.

4. *Pray broadly.* I've been in churches in which the morning prayer has a narrow focus. It sounds like, "Lord, bless us, this service, and the people mentioned in the bulletin." It's like we think God is only interested in what concerns us personally. Think of our Savior who taught us to pray about the kingdom coming, God's will being done, and delivering us all from evil. He has the *whole world* in his mind. Consider "praying the news" so that God's reign may be exhibited in the face of all the violence, injustice, and suffering in our world. The wise worship leader prays with his or her eyes on the needs and the needy of the world around us. Some churches will even extend their prayer ministry for their community, not only faithfully remembering the needs of the community in worship, but soliciting prayer needs from members of the community, making their prayer ministry available to all.

5. *Let your worship prayers exhibit balance.* Wise is the worship leader whose public worship prayers are neither so short that

they say nothing, nor so long they lose everyone's participation. They include both timeless and historic words and contemporary, relevant language that speaks of current needs. They include everyone, even those we don't know about, and are personal enough to rivet the attention of all on particular needs. Both local and worldwide needs should find a place in your prayers.

6. *Borrow the words of others.* We ought not to feel obligated to make all the words and petitions of our prayer our own words. So many others have prayed similar thoughts and may say them more beautifully and descriptively than we can. Feel free to use the Spirit-crafted words of the psalmists or select verses of the epistles. Familiarize yourself with historic prayers that have a timelessness to them. The Calvin Institute of Christian Worship has published *The Worship Sourcebook* in order to make available to us the wisdom and beauty of many such prayers that are part of our Christian heritage.

7. *Pray honestly.* Prayers don't always have to be "nice." Read the psalms and notice how the prayers there are frequently blunt, candid, and earthy. More than half the psalms offer laments, some with strong language and emotion. All this gives us permission to do the same.

So please put your heart into making the worship prayers heartfelt and genuine. The more you do this, the easier it will be for worshipers to enter your prayers with you.

> In need of prayer today?
> We'd love to pray for you.
> Email us at Prayers@[...]church.
> —Seen on a local church signboard

TO PONDER AND DISCUSS

1. Ask several trusted friends how well they remain engaged in the prayers of your worship services. Compare their reactions with your own. If not, how might it be improved?

2. Write a brief description of the purpose of the major morning prayer (or Intercessory Prayer, or Pastoral Prayer). Be sure your description indicates that you have a clear idea of the purpose of such a prayer.

3. How broad or narrow are your prayers in worship? Do they show an awareness of the needs of others in the world? If not, how could you ensure that you include needs beyond your local needs?

Chapter 14

Reading the Bible

I'D LIKE TO BEGIN with a confession. When we pastors retire from the pastorate, many of us impulsively begin to construct a list of "things I'd do differently if I could do it all over again." Mine is quite a list—not deep regrets that point to failure in ministry, but rather perspectives and insights that I gained after stepping back from it all. One of the many items on my list is that I'd include more Bible readings in each worship service, and I'd include them in more intentional ways. I see more and more that we care for people best when we present the Word of God to them thoughtfully and regularly.

The Revised Common Lectionary is an ecumenical, thoughtful, and carefully constructed three-year pattern of Scripture readings for every Sunday of the year, following the Christian calendar. Each Sunday includes an Old Testament reading, followed by a psalm, often sung, a reading from the New Testament epistles, and finally a reading from one of the four Gospels. When followed regularly, worshipers are fed a carefully balanced diet of both testaments, the Psalms, and each of the Gospels.

I have not had the practice of following the Revised Common Lectionary in my ministry. Sometimes I wish I had done so, but at the time, rightly or wrongly, I valued the freedom to make my own Scripture selections based on the theme of the service for the day.

The lectionary just seemed too rigid for me and took away my freedom of choice. It's not that our worship service didn't include regular Bible readings. The greeting, the assurance of pardon, the text for the sermon, and the benediction were always straight from Scripture. But as I look back, I wonder whether my selections seemed a bit scattered, even haphazard. I selected this approach because I wanted to retain the freedom to select passages that seemed most relevant for the theme of the sermon and each part of the liturgy. But now I'm wondering—if we care for people best when we present the Word of God to them thoughtfully and regularly—did I fulfill that task as carefully as I could have.

A variation of the lectionary might be to select passages each week as we craft the worship service, based on the purpose of each part of the service, or the theme of the sermon, or special concerns that are present that day. For example, Psalms 2, 46, and 121 are helpful when crises occur; Psalms 23, 32, and 37 are especially meaningful for those who are distressed, frustrated, or fearful; and deep psalms, such as 10, 13, and 73, are helpful as a lament for those who are questioning and doubting. Whichever method you select, and there are arguments for both, it is important that worshipers be fed a thoughtful and balanced diet of Bible readings.

> God we thank you for your Word,
> the story of your grace.
> —*The Worship Sourcebook*, 148.

Before we enter a consideration of how we can best provide Bible readings, we can well remind ourselves of what is happening when the Bible is read. God reveals himself to us, and through his Spirit he has inspired persons to write his revelation. In his providence he has preserved that inspired Word through the generations. That Word is the primary tool of the Holy Spirit to instruct and form his people. At the same time we might remind ourselves of all that competes against our receiving God's Word. Not only do humans have this inner tendency to turn away from the truth and gather "teachers to say what their itching ears want to hear" (2 Tim 4:3), but our society bombards us with thousands of messages daily, only some of which are reliable and many of which directly contradict what the Bible says. So many who come to worship on Sunday are inevitably wondering, consciously or unconsciously, what must I believe, what is truth, and how can I know what is reliable? Blessed is the pastor and worship leader who will meet folks on Sunday and set before them—faithfully, thoughtfully, and engagingly—the Bible, the only sure Word of God. We care for them best when we do that well.

Some guidelines will direct us in this task:

1. *Present the Word with certainty.* A Bible passage is not merely a special poem or devotional reading by someone; it is the sure Word of God, inspired, certain, and read with authority. So we can introduce the reading with "Hear the Word of the Lord from . . ." and we can end it with "This is the Word of the Lord" and expect them to respond, "Thanks be to God!"

2. *Present the Word with balance.* Though we all have our favorite sections of the Bible that we most easily turn to, be sure that the whole range of the Bible is represented. The strength of the Revised Common Lectionary is that it includes Old Testament passages, Psalms, the Gospels, and the Epistles. And when we consider balance, we will want to ask about whether the passages chosen present only certain characteristics of God and not others. In other words, do they offer a full multifaceted portrayal of God's nature and his acts?

3. *Present the Word for its own purpose.* Wise are those who avoid a utilitarian use of Scripture readings and include a Bible reading because "we need one here in the order of the service." The Word has its own value and its own power. To see "The Old Testament Reading" is reason enough to listen. Similarly with "The New Testament Reading." Each reading has value of its own, aside from its function in the order of service.

4. *Present the Word engagingly.* Readers should prepare well, so they can do justice to the flow of thought and action in the passage. Sometimes multiple voices will be better. Whatever

the method, we should avoid drawing attention to ourselves as readers, on the one hand, and mumbling, on the other hand. Worship planners will want to provide coaching to those who are gifted but need some training to read clearly and with expression.

When Paul left Ephesus he said, "Now I commit you to God and to the word of his grace which can build you up and give you and an inheritance among all those who are sanctified" (Acts 20:32). Surely, we cannot do better than that.

TO PONDER AND DISCUSS

1. How many Scripture readings does your worship service normally have? Can you identify what the purpose is for each? Review a recent worship service, and explain why each passage was selected.

2. Are you familiar with the Revised Common Lectionary? Does your congregation follow it? Why or why not?

3. Evaluate the method of Scripture reading in your worship services. In what ways did the readers help or hinder your efforts to listen? How might that be improved?

Chapter 15

Affirming Our Faith

Generally speaking, those who come to worship are believing people and by coming to worship they are expressing their faith. However, this faith exists on multiple levels. Some people are struggling with the possibility of faith, some have big questions and seek answers, some are young in faith and still being formed, and some are firm in their faith and eager to celebrate. Some believers are surprised that after years of certainty they now find themselves wrestling with doubts. Though much differentiation exists, it is wise for us to plan worship services that, among other things, give us opportunity to verbally express our faith together. To be sure, many of our songs express our faith, but a congregation also needs opportunities to verbalize it.

At times the expression of faith takes on a personal and individualistic character. A new believer may come to be baptized and in the process give a testimony of his or her faith. Previously baptized youths may give expression of their faith, either seeking a welcome to the Lord's Table or becoming a confessing member of the church. Parents make an affirmation of their faith as they present their children to be baptized. Others who have been away from the church for some

> A Three-Sentence Testimony
>
> Christ has died.
> Christ is risen.
> Christ will come again.
>
> —From historic liturgies

time may return and make a reaffirmation of the faith they once embraced. These are all personal expressions of faith in the presence of the congregation of worshipers. As such they should be times of special joy and thanks for all. Planners should carefully incorporate such events into worship, maximizing their benefit for others and honoring God. Songs, prayers, other expressions of thanks and praise will normally accompany them. I hope you have experienced such joy in your congregation.

Sometimes these personal expressions of faith will include thanks for one another. Like Paul, worshipers may say, "I thank my God every time I remember you" (Philippians 1:3). Paul frequently began or ended his epistles with such an expression of thanks for God's work in his audience. We can well learn from his practice. Wise is the church whose worship has times of special celebration for such personal affirmations of faith. At such times the horizontal and the vertical dimensions of worship intersect. "I embrace you as a fellow believer while I give

---

Do you believe in God the Father?
I believe in God, the Father almighty, creator of heaven and earth.

Do you believe in Jesus Christ, the Son of God?
I believe in Jesus Christ, God's only Son, our Lord,
who was conceived by the Holy Spirit,
born of the virgin Mary,
suffered under Pontius Pilate,
was crucified, died, and was buried.
He descended to the dead.
On the third day he rose again;
he ascended into heaven,
he is seated at the right hand of the Father,
and he will come to judge the living and the dead.

Do you believe in God the Holy Spirit?
I believe in the Holy Spirit,
the holy catholic church,
the communion of saints,
the forgiveness of sins,
the resurrection of the body,
and the life everlasting.

—Based on The Apostles' Creed, *The Worship Sourcebook*, 301.

thanks to God for his work in you" is the message we will want to reinforce. While we thankfully recognize God's work in one another, we also affirm our conviction that God is at work in all of us.

At still other times, our affirmations of faith will be corporate, when the entire worshiping congregation becomes one voice. We combine our voices and become one voice toward God and others as we give testimony of our faith. This is perhaps the most common form that our affirmations of faith take. Our testimony is strong as voices are joined together, and our hearts are encouraged as the entire worshiping body makes its affirmation together.

Let's look at a few examples that illustrate how important these affirmations are, when and how they can be done, and the framework in which they should be placed.

A corporate affirmation of faith often uses a creed or confession of the church and is perhaps the most common affirmation of faith. Most frequently congregations will use the words of the Apostle's Creed, another historic creed of the church, or an excerpt from one of the confessions or catechisms of the church. Worshipers might also read one of the psalms of testimony in unison, such as Psalm 23, 116, or 121. Our own creativity will be able to design special professions on the basis of confessional or Scriptural material. Such expressions are both vertical, because we speak to God about our convictions in response to his revelation, and horizontal, because we speak it to one another and to the world around us. Such words provide encouragement to fellow worshipers who may be struggling with their faith, are instructive to the children and youth within the congregation as their faith is formed within them, and also sets before the world where we stand and what our identity is.

In times of crisis and distress, calling the worshipers to express their faith, even amid pain, can offer encouragement, and can serve to form our faith in times of testing. A unison reading of Psalm 46 can be powerfully stabilizing in a time of great uncertainty. Reading Psalm 23 together as an affirmation of faith has given great comfort to those who are grieving. A unison profession of portions of Psalm 103 or 116 can lift the heart of many. And there are many other such possibilities that planners and leaders should keep in mind.

As you plan for such affirmations, keep clearly in mind the needs of the worshiping community, the encouragement needed by those who are discouraged or doubting, formation for children and youth, and the opportunity to offer a testimony to the world.

Who knows what God will do and what good will come when we stand together to affirm our faith?

> My only comfort in life and in death is
> that I am not my own,
> but belong—
> body and soul,
> in life and in death—
> to my faithful Savior Jesus Christ.
> He has fully paid for all my sins with his precious blood,
> and has set me free from the tyranny of the devil.
> He also watches over me in such a way
> that not a hair can fall from my head
> without the will of my Father in heaven:
> in fact, all things must work together for my salvation.
> Because I belong to him,
> Christ, by his Holy Spirit,
> assures me of eternal life
> and makes me wholeheartedly willing and ready
> from now on to live for him.
>
> —"The Heidelberg Catechism," Q&A 1,
> in *Our Faith*, 69–70.

TO PONDER AND DISCUSS

1. Identify the ways in which your worship has recently included affirmations of faith. What was their purpose? To whom were you speaking?

2. Watch the children and youth around you while you are professing. Do they feel free to participate? Muse together on what may be going through their minds. Find opportunity to ask them what it means to them.

3. Cite a recent instance of an affirmation/testimony of faith that was especially meaningful to you. What was it, and why was it so meaningful?

Chapter 16

God Goes with Us

FOR YEARS I NEVER thought deeply about the closing words of a worship service. That moment seemed like turning the key in the door as you left the room. After all, meetings have to come to a close somehow. It was the time to gather Bibles and papers, get the kids' coats on, and head home. Sometimes we listened to the pastor's words, sometimes not!

What a terrible mistake!

Three different types of closing statements are frequently used—a sending, a doxology, and a benediction/blessing. A *sending* is an exhortation to leave with a commitment to obedience—"Go forth to love and serve the Lord." A *doxology* is an exclamation of praise to God for his goodness to us—"To the only God our Savior, be glory, majesty, power, and authority, through Jesus Christ our Lord, before all ages, both now and forever. Amen" (Jude 25). A *benediction/blessing* is a pronouncement of God's loving care such as, "The LORD bless you and keep you; the LORD make his face shine upon you and be gracious unto you; the LORD turn his face toward you and give you peace" (Num 6:24–26) or, "May the grace of the Lord Jesus Christ, and the love of God, and the fellowship of the Holy Spirit be with you all. Amen" (2 Cor 13:14), or some similar passage. While the sending and the doxology may be given by a lay worship leader, the benediction/blessing is properly given by an ordained pastor.

About halfway through my ministry years, I came to realize how profound and rich the third type of statement—the *benediction* or *blessing*—really is! I began to see those words differently as I came to know my parishioners more deeply. I would imagine what might be going on in their hearts (probably in their subconscious). I think the scenario went like this: "It's quiet, comfortable and safe in here, but now I have to go out there and deal with all the pressures of life, all types of temptations, and a world that's determined to sabotage my faith. It's easier to be a Christian here in church than it is to go out there and face it all. But now I must leave . . . and it's scary out there. Can I really be sure that God is with me?" Those moments provide a strategic transition point. Just as my faith led me to affirm that God is willing to meet me here in worship, now by faith I hold to the truth that he will be with me as I leave here. As a matter of fact, I believe that at no point in my journey will he be absent from me.

A pastor has the incredible privilege of standing before the congregation and giving the God-sent promise that gives worshipers exactly what their hearts need—assurance that God will indeed be with them; give them grace, mercy, and peace; and bless and keep them. A pastor says those words not as a wish, or hope, or even a prayer, but as a promise from God from his Word. As the years passed those closing moments of worship became touching (and emotional) moments for me. What a privilege it was to look all these worshipers in the eye and know that, regardless of what they were struggling with, I could

> "Dear friends, the God who holds you in his unbreakable grip goes with you. Hear his promise:
>
> 'The LORD bless you
> and keep you;
> the LORD make his face shine upon you
> and be gracious to you;
> the LORD turn his face toward you
> and give you peace.'"
>
> —A pastor's introduction of the Aaronic Benediction of Numbers 6:24–26.

assure them that God would be their companion all week! I reminded them on occasion that when the original Aaronic Blessing was given in Numbers 6:24–26, God was making it so clear he was identifying with the Israelites that he even said he was putting his name on them to bless them. That underscored the beauty of the moment even more.

> When asked how she liked her new pastor, a woman enthusiastically replied, "Oh, he is wonderful. He gives the best benedictions! . . . His benedictions have become the highlight of each Sunday as far as I am concerned."
>
> —William Willimon, *Worship as Pastoral Care*, 210.

Many worshipers gained that same deep appreciation for that closing. They came to see themselves as benediction-people, people who went into the week with God's companionship. Benediction-people have a greater sense of peace and security; they are more aware of the presence of God in their life; and they remind themselves of those words when the going gets particularly tough. They had not only received God's care during the time of worship, but such care would go with them as they left.

Wise are the worship leaders who are clear about these two considerations:

- For the benediction or blessing to be received as God's pronouncement, the words used should be either directly scriptural or a close paraphrase of Scripture's promises. It will not be received in quite the same way if the words are casual or ad lib.

- In the Reformed tradition, the clergyperson usually gives this blessing with upraised hands as an official act of ministry, indicating this blessing from God being pronounced on them is assured.

Once we grasp the beauty of God's blessing on us, we find other ways to share the same comfort. I've talked to parents who speak these words of benediction to their young children as they tuck them into bed at night. I find it special to pronounce these words on a person, young or old, who has just been baptized, on youth who have just professed their faith in Christ, on a young couple at the close of their wedding ceremony, on a person who is dying, and on a grieving family at the close of a funeral service.

So in worship God has the last word! I can't think of deeper care to give than the assurance that God has placed his name on those who have gathered!

TO PONDER AND DISCUSS

1. Do your worship services end with a pronounced *benediction/blessing*? If not, why not? If so, how much attention do most folks pay to it? How could that be improved?

2. Describe what it means to you to receive God's blessing each week. In what way does it make a difference to you?

3. Do you clearly understand the difference between a "sending," a "doxology," and a "blessing"? Discuss these differences with others close to you. Who is the agent in each? The recipient?

PART THREE

Special Occasions in the Liturgy

IN ADDITION TO THE common elements of worship we have examined in part 2, other events in worship are included only on occasion. Some may appear seldom, and some on a regular basis, though not weekly. Some can be anticipated a short time ahead, but some, such as crises, are unexpected. For example, on some weeks a baptism may be requested, or it may seem wise to affirm and remember our baptisms, or the Lord's Supper is to be commemorated. At other times the congregation is impacted by a time of crisis, and great pain may call for a time of lament and prayers on challenging issues. And of course, there are funerals and weddings, which will likely be scheduled on a weekday but nevertheless ought to be considered worship events.

These occasional and special events often challenge worship planners, who may have grown accustomed to the regular/normal liturgy. Therefore they need special attention so they convey the same caring as the weekly liturgy. As worship planners and leaders therefore we must be prepared, yet flexible and empathetic.

Chapter 17

When Crises Arise

IN ADDITION TO ALL the usual needs that worshipers bring with them to worship, they are sometimes rocked by a crisis that brings searing pain and tears, shaking their foundation. Should we make room for such feelings in worship?

While on vacation recently, I worshiped at a local Presbyterian church. As I entered, I was surprised to find each row had a Bible, a hymnal, and a box of tissue. I was puzzled because I'd never seen that before, and I wondered if it could be a heavy allergy season. But then it hit me—these boxes of tissue carry their own message: "It's OK to cry in this church. We understand life involves pain and disappointment."

Three kinds of crises can disrupt an otherwise praise-filled worship service. First, there are *personal crises,* the kind that worshipers bring with them—a family or marriage in turmoil, a broken heart, guilt feelings, depression, broken relationships, or seething anger. There are also *corporate crises,* the kind that affect virtually the entire body of worshipers. I had to announce at the opening of worship one Sunday that a high school basketball star, one of our leading youths, had been killed the night before in an accident caused by a drunk driver. Another time, a young mother had suddenly died of a heart attack at a local campground. Worship can hardly proceed as usual after receiving such information.

And there are also *communitywide crises,* those caused by events with wide-ranging impact. A tornado hits parts of town, for instance. We all remember the September 11, 2001 attacks, racial tensions and violence in our cities, the tsunami that devastated the Philippines in 2013, and hurricanes in the Gulf Coast. We cannot ignore such events in worship.

Each of these creates a challenge for worship leaders. They need wisdom and discernment to determine whether worship should be reshaped and, if so, how extensively. Blessed are the worship planners and leaders who have established relationships of trust and collaboration so they can deal with these unexpected circumstances together.

Worship planners and leaders usually have four options available:

- Some may want to do nothing and proceed with the worship service as planned. This may be legitimate if the planners are convinced that what has happened has no appreciable impact on the congregation as a whole. But it's risky. It may send out the message that "we just do our own worship here and let the rest of society go on its own way" or worse yet, "We don't care."

- The second option is to make only slight changes to the liturgy. For example, the morning prayer may be focused more on the needs of the day and intercession for those who are affected; or the worship leader may include some appropriate meditative thoughts from Scripture introduced with comments such as "even if you are not affected directly, this event matters because we are all, worldwide, brothers and sisters." An appropriate song, or a litany of Scripture, may assist the worshipers in giving expression to their concerns, pain, and pleas. These are added to what has been planned, but the remainder of the service remains intact.

- In some instances it may be wise to make more extensive changes in the liturgy. An entire section of the service, for instance, might be set aside to give leaders and the congregation an opportunity to reflect on the crisis, express their shock and pain, offer intercessions, grieve together, and uphold their faith in our benevolent God.

- Sometimes nothing short of a complete revision of the service of worship will be appropriate. For worship planners, setting aside a previously planned service on Friday or Saturday may be upsetting, even if it is necessary. Such circumstances do not arise often, but we must be prepared for them. I can think of three instances in which this happened in my ministry. A young mother who was a dearly loved leader had fought cancer for a number of years. All rejoiced that she was doing so well, but suddenly her disease took a violent turn and on Thursday she passed away. The congregation who loved her and had cared for her so well needed a time to grieve, pray, and reflect. At another time, a terrible auto accident tragically disrupted an outing of the church's seniors group. Death and critical injuries resulted, and the congregation was traumatized. The "usual" worship service would not fit that Sunday morning. And we can all remember how churches quickly put away their liturgies planned for the Sunday morning after September 11, 2001. We were stunned, scared, and grieving. We needed worship that took all of this into account. To continue with a previously-planned worship service without acknowledging the crisis that occurred could

---

Evaluating the severity of crises and their impact on worship:

LEVEL ONE—Only a small number of worshipers are affected.

Minor modifications to the liturgy are made.

LEVEL TWO—The event has potentially a major impact on a larger number, perhaps nearly half, of worshipers.

A new and pastorally appropriate worship service is planned.

LEVEL THREE—The event has a profound and long-term impact on a nearly all in a worshiping community.

Worship leaders give long-term (multiple weeks) attention to the needs of worshipers.

—Howard Vanderwell

send out a message that our worship isn't really concerned about such things.

The degree to which the service ought to be modified will be determined by the severity of the impact of the crisis on the congregation. Careful discernment by wise leaders is obviously needed here. At times you may want to devote a series of services to ministering to a particular longer-tem need. There are, of course, dangers involved. A sense of cohesiveness and unity within the service can be lost, selections of songs and passages are made with less thoughtfulness, and the planners lose sight of the overall impact of the service.

In such instances, you have six building blocks that can be combined to provide worship that cares in a time of crisis.

1. *Music*—Wise is the musician who will provide service music that never does violence to a grieving heart and soul, but rather gives an opportunity to grieve, reflect, and breathe in the Spirit of God.

2. *Songs*—A grieving congregation needs to sing. But strong uplifting praise songs can be offensive to the hurting heart. Blessed is the congregation whose leaders and musicians can choose songs that express our grief, intercessions, and yearning for hope.

3. *Prayers*—Sensitive, caring, and passionate prayers will help worshipers raise their pleas to God for help, strength, and faith, and hold up those who are suffering. At the same time these prayers always express our faith in God as ruler over all. Maybe it will be appropriate for several people to lead in prayer, or at times, for the entire congregation to offer what is sometimes called a concert of prayer, that is, small groups turning toward each other for prayer in their pews.

4. *Words*—Let God's Word—rich with its promises of security, candid with its laments, and lofty in its view of this world as totally in God's hand—be the food for our souls. Read

appropriate Scripture passages, and reflect on them, but understand that people in stress will have a limited concentration span.

5. *Laments*—Now is the time to do what we often find difficult to do—to honestly and openly express our pain, struggles, and even big questions to God. We learn from the psalms that God gives us permission to do so. Our painful concerns may be expressed in the prayer, or the reading of psalms of lament, or perhaps in a lament written for the occasion.

6. *Actions of Service*—Sometimes a healthy response to a crisis can take the form of caring for others in the community. For example, when a tornado strikes, we can call to God in worship and then go help neighbors clean up the mess after worship or take a special offering of some sort for relief efforts.

May you have an awareness that will help you discern what events impact your worshipers, wisdom to discern what their needs are, and a spirit of loving care that enables you to respond helpfully.

Primary tools for worship in time of crisis:
- Scripture passages that express pain
- Corporate expressions/readings of lament
- Music and song for expression and affirmation
- Proclamation of promises to provide support
- Music and songs that express our thoughts, feelings, and faith
- Sermons that speak to the hurting heart
- Affirmations and testimonies about experiences of God's special care
- Intercessory prayers
- Actions of service to aid others in need

—Howard Vanderwell

TO PONDER AND DISCUSS

1. How would it strike you to find a box of tissue in the pew at church? Is that appropriate? Why or why not?

2. Cite an instance when events during the week required that worship for Sunday morning be modified. How was that done?

3. What are the dangers of making major modifications to a worship service? How should worship planners make those decisions?

Chapter 18

Receiving Our Identity in Baptism

BAPTISM, RATHER THAN BEING a private or family event, is one of those special events in the worship life of a congregation that requires careful attention. It's a time to celebrate God's grace, to focus on his promises, and to give thanks for new life in Christ.

I have in mind here baptism in three situations—(1) covenant infants, that is, those who are born to believing parents and therefore considered members of God's covenant arrangement, (2) adults who have come to faith and had not previously been baptized, and (3) unbaptized children of parents who have recently come to faith. In some congregations most baptisms will be infant baptisms. In others, believer's baptisms may take place regularly. In each of these situations the spirit and tone of the service will require careful attention, though the basic truths are the same.

The importance of baptism services in the life of a worshiping congregation cannot be overestimated. In baptism:

- The covenant promises of God are extended.

- His covenant is celebrated.

- Those who receive the sacrament in faith receive God's grace.

- Those who receive the sacrament in faith are given their identity in Christ.

- Our status as a member of the body of Christ is affirmed.
- We are reminded of our calling to follow Christ.
- The nature of the Christian congregation is illustrated.

Each of these is worthy of careful attention in a baptism service.

It is important that we not only *do* the baptism, but also that it is carried out in a manner that will inspire others and nurture the faith and understanding of all who are present. So our focus here will be on the manner in which the sacrament is presented, rather than on the theological understanding of the event. We must all aim for caring baptisms!

When Ben was baptized, women from the congregation had made a small banner to be hung on the baptism font. "Ben—Child of God" it boldly said. After the baptism, the banner was presented to his family. For years it hung on the wall of Ben's bedroom. "Ben—Child of God" was always clearly before him as his identity was shaped.

—Used by permission

A baptism service should carry deep meaning for all who are present—the family, guests, and worshipers of all ages. Here is an opportunity to administer a sacred rite in a way that enhances and reinforces the caring spirit of the liturgy for all.

The congregation and worship leaders who consider these suggested guidelines will find baptisms nurture the faith of all who are witnesses.

1. *Make the rite a time of celebration.* The manner of the liturgy and the spirit of those who preside should clearly communicate a sense of joy and privilege. Never is baptism merely an obligation we must fulfill. Blessed is the worshiping community that senses the spirit of celebration at each baptism service.

2. *Keep the focus on God.* Baptism is the act of a gracious covenant God who is extending his promises of love and care to a child or adult. The focus, therefore, is on the grace and

faithfulness of God, rather than on the cute baby or exemplary family. Baptism is built on the conviction that God is the first mover and we are responders.

3. *Include the children of the congregation.* It is important that children observe the baptism closely for each new baptism is an opportunity for them to remember their own and better understand its importance. In the congregation I last served, the young children of the congregation (and there were many) were invited to join the pastor at the front of the sanctuary for the baptism. Personal words were spoken to them about their baptism, and they could observe the baptism up close.

4. *Celebrate the family circle.* While the family is secondary to God's role, here is an opportunity to highlight the value of a faithful covenant family in God's design. When multiple generations are bound together in commitment to one another and a new generation, we see the value of a stable family circle.

5. *Include words of encouragement and challenge to the children and youth.* Baptism is God's free gift to us, but it always calls for a response on our part as we grow and mature. A tactful and sensitive reminder to the children and youth of the congregation about their response is appropriate to nurture their faith.

6. *Provide a baptism symbol.* Some tangible symbol of the baptism given to the parents for their home can be used to regularly remind a growing child, "I am baptized." It may be a candle, a banner, a piece of art or sculpture, or something similar that can be visible in a child's room. A congregation may also give the family a video of the baptism service for later viewing.

7. *Be sensitive to single parents.* There are multiple reasons for a child to be presented for baptism by one parent. A congregation should not be judgmental toward the family, but rather be encouraged to support a single parent who takes on the large task of parenthood alone.

8. *Highlight the congregational vows of support and caring.* Congregational vows are not just a routine part of the sacrament, but rather a momentous time when a whole congregation takes a vow to accept, love, support, and pray for a child. Such a corporate act should be given a place in the liturgy worthy of such importance. The commitment of the congregation should be held up as a gift to be cherished by parents, children, and youth alike.

9. *Remembering parents in pain.* In every congregation there are parents who grieve because they have children who are not faithful to their baptism. Baptism services are particularly painful for these folks. Their pain should not be ignored, but somewhere in the baptism service words of encouragement or prayers of intercession should be offered for such families.

10. *Thanks to mentors.* All who are baptized need mentors to guide them in their growth. Some churches wisely include sponsors/godparents. Infants need many teachers and encouragers in the faith along the way. Those who come to faith as adults need companions to guide them on the journey of a growing faith. Such work is often done quietly and goes unrecognized. Yet, a baptism service is an ideal time to acknowledge such efforts and offer words of thanks and encouragement.

Rich is the congregation that has the frequent privilege of baptism services, and richer yet is the congregation where such liturgies are marked by sensitive caring and encouragement. When you plan a baptism service, put your best efforts into it!

Baptism in an Adoptive Family

A family with three adolescent children has adopted two children and now presents the two adopted children for baptism. To integrate the entire family into the formation process, the following adaptation of the baptism service was used. After the parents had responded to the baptismal question by which they expressed their

---

faith commitment and their vows to care for these two children, the entire family gathered as the following questions were asked:

To the Adolescent Siblings

Do you as siblings of _____ and _____ accept them as your brother and sister, and will you love them and participate in their growth and formation?

We do, God helping us.

To the Congregation

This is _____ and _____, children of God, entrusted to _____ as their earthly parents and to us as a congregation. Will you receive them in love, pray for them, and help instruct them in the Christian faith?

We will, God helping us.

Will you encourage and support these parents as they train them in the ways of the Lord, and also these siblings as they encourage them?

We will, God helping us.

THE BAPTISM

_____, I baptize you in the name of the Father, the Son, and the Holy Spirit. Amen.

—Used by permission

THE BLESSING

(After the water of baptism has been administered, the pastor shall place his hand on each child and shall say)

_____, for you Jesus Christ came into the world:

for you he lived and showed God's love;

for you he suffered the darkness of Calvary

and cried at last, "It is finished";

for you he triumphed over death

and rose in newness of life;

for you he ascended to reign at God's right hand.

All this he did for you, _____,

before you knew anything of it.

And so the Word of Scripture is fulfilled:

"We love because God loved us first."

—*The Worship Sourcebook*, 281.

TO PONDER AND DISCUSS

1. How frequently does your congregation have baptism services? If often, do they seem routine? How could you make them more "caring" for the entire congregation?

2. Review the ten guidelines given above. Which receive attention in your congregation and ministry? Which need more attention? How could you do that?

3. Talk to several children and youth (middle school and high school) and ask them what they notice in a baptism service and how they feel about their own baptism after such a service.

Chapter 19

Remembering Our Baptism

PREVIOUSLY, WE REFLECTED ON the joy of celebrating baptisms in the life of a congregation. However, we must also acknowledge that churches, especially those that practice infant baptisms, may have a problem. It's the problem of unintentionally forgetting our baptism—failing to keep the memory of our baptism alive. Those baptized as infants or young children cannot be expected to keep a lively memory of something that happened when they were too young to understand it or even have any memory of it. Even those baptized as adults find some of its joy fading over time. Consequently, one of the needs of worshipers, though perhaps unrealized, is to make their baptism a greater reality in their faith life. Since we receive our identity in Christ at our baptism, it will be healthy and healing to be reminded regularly of our baptismal identity. People who long for a sense of belonging to the body of Christ need such a reminder.

Churches, therefore, in addition to baptism, also need times when they intentionally affirm or remember those baptisms. True, this task takes place in two other settings: in the home, where parents form the faith of their children by reminding them of their baptism, and in a church education class, where the youth of the church are instructed in the meaning of baptism. It is also true that every time we witness the baptism of another person, it is a fit reminder of our own. Yet something more is needed. And so we suggest that the life of a congregation will be enriched when the liturgy regularly calls all those baptized to remember and affirm their baptism. Such worship times will supplement (and encourage) the efforts of parents and also reinforce the efforts of church education.

Some of those reminders will be stirred by a visible font. Wise is the church that has a prominent baptism font always visible in the sanctuary. Even a service in which no baptism takes place the font conveys the unspoken message that "baptized people worship here." In some churches, the font is placed in the narthex or at the beginning of a wide center aisle to communicate that entrance to the church is through the waters of baptism. Churches that practice adult baptism by immersion do well, if at all possible, to keep the baptistery visible.

Thoughtful worship leaders will refer to baptism at appropriate places in the liturgy. The call to worship may remind worshipers that just as Israel journeyed to the promised land through the waters of the Red Sea, so we continue our journey as those who have been cleansed through the waters of baptism. When we are called to confess our sins, a reminder of the waters of our baptism provides an assurance of our forgiveness. A similar reference is appropriate when the assurance of pardon is given.

Many are the special events in the life of a congregation that afford us an excellent opportunity for us to recall our

Ted and Sara have three children, two daughters and a son. At the children's baptisms they were each given a large white baptism candle and encouraged to light it on the children's baptism birthday. As a family they developed the practice of having a special family meal on each baptism birthday with the lit candle in the center of the table. At the close of the meal the parents read the story of Jesus' baptism from the Gospels and then told the story of baptism Sunday for each child. The children never tired of hearing these stories and eagerly looked forward to each other's baptism remembrance.

—Used by permission.

baptism—when youth make a profession of their faith, when new members are received, one returns to church after a period of absence, a congregational anniversary is observed, a new pastor is installed, or the Lord's Supper is commemorated. But more personal events also provide opportunities. When couples prepare to exchange marriage vows and begin with a reminder of their identity in Christ proclaimed at their baptism or when a life is remembered at a funeral or memorial service, worshipers can be reminded that this life began at the baptism font years ago, when identity in Christ was established.

Even more memorable will be those special occasions when all worshipers are not only reminded of their baptisms, but are called to repeat and reaffirm the vows made at baptism, whether they were first spoken by an adult or, in the case of an infant, they were implicit in the baptism and wait for expression when maturity comes. In either case worshipers are called to publicly affirm those vows, thereby highlighting their significance in the mind and heart of each person.

There are two ways in which this can be done. A portion of the liturgy can be set aside as an affirmation of baptism in much the same way that a portion of the liturgy is dedicated to baptism, profession of faith, ordination of office-bearers, and the like. The intent is clearly explained to the worshipers, and they are asked to stand and affirm their original baptismal vows. Adding such a segment to the liturgy will be most meaningful

> "These liturgies . . . should be celebrated so as to communicate both that they are connected to the church's celebration of baptism and that they do not repeat a baptism. Services that include remembrance of baptism should also be intentional about welcoming not only those who have a baptism to remember but also those who do not. In fact, the main goal of the remembrance of baptism should be to proclaim the gospel so directly, sincerely, and enthusiastically that spiritual seekers will more eagerly anticipate their own baptism."
>
> —*The Worship Sourcebook*, 291.

when it is coupled with a companion event, such as the baptism of another, a profession of faith, the welcome of new members, and so forth.

A more notable effort would be to make an entire service a time of affirmation of our baptism. When you establish the worship schedule for the year, worship leaders could include a Sunday of baptismal affirmation. The theme of the service, the message of the sermon, prayers, and songs all can point toward the need for recommitment in our Christian journey. Such a service should be explained ahead of time so that those who come are prepared. I've had contact with a congregation that made every first Sunday of the New Year "Affirmation Sunday,"

> Suggested vow for affirmation of baptism
> Trusting in the gracious promises of God, do you renounce sin and the power of evil in your life and the world?
> **I renounce them.**
> Who is your Lord and Savior?
> **Jesus Christ is my Lord and Savior.**
> Will you be Christ's faithful disciple, obeying his Word and showing his love?
> **God being my helper, I will.**
> —*Lift Up Your Hearts*, 848. Additional ideas are found in *The Worship Sourcebook*, 289ff.

In both of these efforts, the vows of affirmation and the entire liturgy can be found in *Lift Up Your Hearts*[1] or other service books. Additional ideas are found in *The Worship Sourcebook*.[2] One reminder is in order, however. An affirmation of baptism is *not* an occasion for re-baptism. Baptism is a one-time event, and

1. *Lift Up Your Hearts: Psalms, Hymns, and Spiritual Songs* (Grand Rapids: Faith Alive Christian Resources, 2013).

2. *The Worship Sourcebook*, 2nd ed. (Grand Rapids: Calvin Institute of Christian Worship and Faith Alive Christian Resources, 2013).

God's promises at baptism are valid for all time. An affirmation of baptism can, instead, be a way to satisfy an individual's desire for re-baptism.

Worshipers generally need a sense of belonging. And in this age of individualism such a longing often goes unfulfilled. Baptism and the remembering of it affirm our inclusion as members of the body of Christ, thereby deepening our confidence of our acceptance by God and by others.

TO PONDER AND DISCUSS

1. Have you ever experienced the affirmation or remembering of your baptism? If so, what did it mean to you? If not, what benefits from it can you imagine?

2. How often is baptism referred to in your worship services, apart from actual baptism services?

3. How would you respond if someone in your planning team suggested an annual affirmation of baptism service? Why would you respond that way?

Chapter 20

Nurture at the Table

I WONDER WHAT KIND of questions come to your mind when it's time to plan a service of the Lords' Supper. I've observed that churches often have a lot of confusion about the Lord's Supper (regardless of whether we name it Communion, The Lord's Supper, or the Eucharist). In addition to the theological questions about how Christ is present in the meal, there are other more practical questions. How often should we schedule it? Should children partake? Should participants receive the elements in the pew or come forward, by intinction, or in some other way? Should we come in a spirit of thanks or sorrow? Is it merely a memorial, or do we really meet Christ here? How should we prepare to come?

But there is also uncertainty about just what we should expect to receive from our celebration of the Lord's Supper. Some, I fear, expect little except to have participated in a memorial about Christ. They are satisfied that they have remembered. So much more ought to happen, however. And a church with a caring worship life will form worshipers who come with a spirit of expectancy, knowing there are great gifts waiting for us here! We will be fed well!

The Reformed Confessions spell out what we may expect. The Belgic Confession of Faith (art.35) speaks of the nurture we can expect to receive. I encourage you to read that before you plan a liturgy of the Lord's Supper. We have two lives in us, we are told.

One is earthly and physical; the other is spiritual and heavenly. Both need to be supported and nurtured. To do so for our physical life, we regularly eat physical food. And to support our spiritual life, God has given us the living bread, namely Jesus Christ. It follows then, that in both we can expect to leave the Table having been fed well. With our stomachs we receive physical bread, and with our faith we receive Jesus Christ the living bread. We come with an appetite, and we leave satisfied. That's far different from coming to merely remember someone or something.

Similarly, the Heidelberg Catechism[1] uses terminology that points to much the same kind of emphasis. Notice how the "nourish and nurture" concepts surface regularly and with strength. In Q/A 77 Christ is said to "nourish and refresh" believers with his body and blood. In Q/A 79 the catechism says that Christ wants to teach us that his crucified body and shed blood are "the true food and drink of our souls for eternal life." And again it says he wants to assure us that we do surely "share in his true body and blood."

These words indicate we are sharing a life-giving and health-inducing meal. There is no reference here to a mere memorial. Here we are enjoined to come with expectancy, with a sense of our need for nurture, feeding, and assurance, and with confidence that we will leave healthier than when we came. This sacrament is, therefore, for people who are weak and needy, and who desire to be healed and fed—to be strengthened.

One day a pastor was reflecting on his church's commemoration of the Lord's Supper. Their practice called for a

> The late Robert Webber was running late for our 1:00 appointment in his office. We were waiting patiently in the hallway outside his office when he came hurrying down the hallway. "I'm so sorry to be late," he said, "but I was stopped by a troubled student who needed some attention." When we explained that we fully understood, his response was, "You know what I told him? Flee to the Eucharist! That's what I told him. Flee to the Eucharist!"
>
> —Howard Vanderwell

1. "The Heidelberg Catechism," in *Our Faith*, 69.

small group of worshipers to come forward, gather at a table in turn, and partake. After one of those services another member of the congregation said to this pastor, "Hey, did you notice that everyone at the table this morning had experienced a real tragedy in their life within the past five years?" In his mind, the pastor reviewed the stories there—death, disease, family conflict, bruises, and wounds. Outwardly they were young and old, rich and poor, educated and not. But as they raised the cup and ate the bread they were all exactly the same—broken, hurting, lost people who came to the table for healing and nurture. And then the pastor explained, "We all limp to this table, and we are forgiven and united again to the Savior's family." The message is clear—this Table is for those who limp!

Sharing the Lord's Supper is a powerful experience for those who come in that spirit and with that kind of expectancy. Therefore, those of us who plan worship and those who lead it must invest sensitive pastoral caring in services of the Lord's Supper. This is not merely a memorial. It is a time to meet our Savior, who knows our neediness and wants to nurture us.

In your work, then, consider these guidelines for services of the Lords' Supper that will be nurturing and caring.

> "This is our story. This is who we all are. Whatever affinities and distinctions your outer markings show, *we all limp to this table.* Some of us limp in Brookes Brothers, others in Birkenstocks, but we all limp. And at this table Jesus says to us, 'This is my body, take and eat, your sins are forgiven, you are my family.'"
>
> —A Pastor

1. Let the elders, worship planners, and pastors plan and approach these services of worship with a holy sense of awe. When we come to the table (to plan, to lead, or to partake) we are standing on holy ground. It's more than a memorial. Christ aims to meet his limping children and nourish them toward eternal life.

2. Keep the children and the youth in view. They are not spectators. This is not merely a "mysterious rite" they do not yet

understand. We should use visuals and gestures that are accessible to the children. Let liturgists explain the sacrament in non-technical language that is accessible to children and youth. Let parents explain while in the pew with them. Even if they do not commune, let the pastor welcome them with a blessing. In all things, aim to stir within the children and youth the desire to be fed and cared for.

3. Put no obstacles in the way. Perhaps some people need gluten-free bread to fully participate. Let us provide it willingly. Some may have mobility problems and need assistance. Even those who are shut-in should be included with home communion.

4. Passing the peace during the sacrament is an act that symbolizes both the bond we have with each other and the gift we have received from Christ. People with Christ's peace extend it in love to one another. Far better than saying "Good morning" is assuring one another, "The peace of Christ to you."

5. Seek to practice holy leisure at the table. To feel rushed and hurry through the service will contradict the spirit Christ intends. Let there be no rush to "get done on time." Let us all have the luxury of lingering, perhaps with a time of silence, while we reflect on the gifts of Christ and our time of meeting him face to face.

6. Expect to leave with a thankful faith. We have met Christ. We have been fed. We are nurtured. In spite of our weaknesses and our limping, we are accepted in Christ. There is, then, one way to leave—grateful, healthier, and intent on serving our Lord.

The early Christians often called the Lord's Supper a lovefeast. While celebrating the love of Christ given to them, they found new hope, strength, and assurance. At the same time they renewed their bond with one another as members of the body of Christ.

TO PONDER AND DISCUSS

1. When you come to the Lord's Table, do you come with expectancy? If so, what do you expect to happen? If not, what would help to stir your expectancy?

2. What are your earliest childhood memories of the Lord's Supper? How did you feel about the sacrament? How do your thoughts and feelings about it differ now?

3. Think of the last few times your congregation observed the Lord's Supper. Was your heart any different afterwards than before? If so, how? If not, how could this be changed, so the next time it will be different?

Chapter 21

When We Need to Cry

I'M SURE YOU'VE HEARD it often—worship is praising God! And we are told, "Let's just praise God with all our hearts today." And we are exhorted, "Come now, we can sing these praises better than that this morning." Too often worship and praise are equated. "No praise, no worship," they say.

But what about those who can't praise God? What about those whose hearts are too heavy to muster up praise today? There are times when I have felt violated when I was told that we should all be praising God. Maybe that's true in general, but I couldn't do it that day. What about people who feel like that? And what about those times when tragedy strikes the congregation? What about those whose hearts are too heavy to praise? What about all those times when we need to cry instead?

While praise is, indeed, a major part of worshiping God, it is not the only expression God desires. And to demand praise in spite of our need to cry can force us into dishonest worship. In worship, God welcomes us as we are. So it is important that we think more broadly about the different experiences that shape our worship and, among others, we should re-examine the role of lament. If worship aims to promote a spirit of caring then it also needs to include the right to lament at times. Certainly many psalms are psalms of praise and provide a stirring model for us.

But not all are praise. Bernhard W. Anderson says, "Laments far outnumber any other kind of songs in the Psalter."[1] Job, Lamentations, and sections of Jeremiah contain lament as well. Yet, have you ever encountered a church with a "lament team"?

> "How long, O LORD? Will you forget me forever?
> How long will you hide your face from me?
> How long must I wrestle with my thoughts
> And every day have sorrow in my heart?
> How long will my enemy triumph over me?
> Look on me and answer, O LORD my God.
> Give light to my eyes, or I will sleep in death;
> My enemy will say, "I have overcome him,"
> And my foes will rejoice when I fall."
>
> —Psalm 13:1–4

Keep these thoughts in mind:

- Life for all of us includes the experience of pain and disappointment. Worship, therefore, that welcomes us as we are will necessarily include an expression of these feelings.

- Laments contain key convictions that are central to healthy worship. They are shaped by the assumption that God and his Word comes to us in the midst of life, including its suffering. He is open to our cries, and he intends to help those who are oppressed.

- Laments give us permission to be honest and candid with God, with no need to suppress our pain when we come into his presence.

- Yet, we always cry out in the context of faith, so after we have expressed an earthy and candid complaint, we also affirm the truth that God is trustworthy and faithful. He does care for

---

1. Anderson, *Out of the Depths*, 66.

us and his hand will hold us, so we are free to call on him for help.

- Laments express our confidence that God can handle all our thoughts and feelings. He does not expect us to stifle our pain, our cries for help, even our complaints and anger.

We find that some laments in Scripture are individual cries of one person who finds the trials of life so overwhelming that they stir up a cry for help. Other laments come out of a community when life is hard and they find it difficult to believe that God is with them.

An awareness of the presence of laments in Scripture is necessary preparation for all of us who plan and lead worship. It will protect us from a false worship that insists we may only express praise to God. It will deepen our solidarity with God's children in other generations who cried to God in both pain and faith, and who expressed to him both their trust and their hard, even angry, questions. It will help us feel and practice compassion for our neighbors who suffer, whether next door or around the globe. And it will enable us to be more empathetic to the trials and difficulties that many others may be experiencing. For example:

> "No experience in life is too difficult to be brought before God."
> —*The Worship Sourcebook*, 111

- If David could cry, "How long, O LORD, will you forget me forever? How long will you hide your face from me?" (Ps 13:1), can we not do the same?

- If Asaph can pray. "This is what the wicked are like—always carefree, they increase in wealth. Surely in vain have I kept my heart pure; in vain have I washed my hands in innocence," (Ps 73:12–13), then surely we can raise our complaints with God too.

- If Israel gathered in worship and cried, "Restore us, O God; make your face shine upon us, that we may be saved. O LORD

God Almighty, how long will your anger smolder against the prayers of your people?" (Ps 80:3–4), then might we hear the same in a worship prayer today?

There is something therapeutic in the act of expressing our deep pain to God, rather than thinking we must deny and bury it all the time. And healing comes from the God who cares for us when we endure trials and who does hear our cries for help. No congregation should be deprived of these benefits.

Obviously, laments should be incorporated in public worship cautiously and in a balanced manner. Not all psalms are lament; not all prayers should lament. Laments and cries should not replace praise and thanks, but provide a balance to them. Wise are the worship planners and leaders who can discern when there are legitimate reasons for laments and sense how and when to express them.

Generally, four parts of the worship service are the most suitable times for lament.

- *Sermon.* Lament can and should be expressed in the sermon, especially when reflecting on pain and suffering. Naming the questions and complaints we have can be permission-giving and encourage listeners to be more open in their private conversations with God. It will also strengthen the spirits of those who have come with hurting hearts.

- *Scripture readings.* It is wise to have multiple Scripture readings in a worship service and to include various types of passages. To include occasional laments, with a word of explanation, can provide a healthy balance to passages of praise, thanks, or confession.

- *Prayers.* Prayers are the most likely place to offer lament. In public prayers we gather up the needs of others and express them to God. If we are honest in our praying, our needs and complaints must be included. The events of the week and the severity of the trials will determine how strongly they are expressed.

- *Songs.* In many locations in our liturgies songs of praise and thanks are natural. But in other locations, particularly near our prayers, even surrounding our prayers, songs of lament are needed. The repertoire of a congregation must include each.

> "The Bible prefigures a tenet of modern psychology: you can't really deny your feelings or make them disappear, so you might as well express them. God can deal with every human response save one. He cannot abide the response I fall back on instinctively: an attempt to ignore him or treat him as though he does not exist."
>
> —Philip Yancey, *Disappointment with God,* 235

Since most worshipers will expect and need to be comforted and inspired in Sunday worship, we may experience some resistance to the inclusion of laments. Such worshipers might prefer not to be reminded of pain and suffering while they worship. It is wise, therefore, to use them with a clear reason for doing so. But their inclusion may also require some explanation about why they are appropriate.

TO PONDER AND DISCUSS

1. Are laments expressed in your worship services? If not, why not? If so, how often? How strongly? Do you think most worshipers understand why they are necessary? Do you think some worshipers will object to being so honest and candid with God and would prefer that all prayers, for instance, be nice and polite? What would lead them to that feeling?

2. Is it possible some educational efforts are necessary to help your congregation understand the role and necessity of laments? How can that be done?

3. How can we help people who need to lament also affirm their faith that, though their pain has no neat theological and rational explanations, they can still rest in God as the one who is ultimately in control and still cares for them?

Chapter 22

Prayers on Challenging Issues

PRAYERS HAVE A BIG part in our liturgies. Each has a specific purpose and focus, but one prayer is generally considered to be the primary intercessory prayer of the worship service. You may call it the pastoral prayer, or the morning prayer, or the prayers of the people, or something else. It is the time when the personal and pastoral needs of the congregation are gathered and held up to God for his attention. Those who lead these prayers will aim to be aware of the needs within the worshiping community and incorporate them into the prayer petitions.

But you may find that some of these prayers are challenging to craft, because they deal with sensitive issues. Some of these issues may involve matters of privacy or may be matters on which a difference of opinion exists in the congregation. If not dealt with wisely and discerningly, they can become either controversial and offensive or bland and banal. So worship leaders need to be alert to these issues ahead of time. (You will find additional helpful suggestions in *The Worship Sourcebook*.) We suggest three areas for your consideration.

One of the issues is *personal privacy*. Prayers in public worship are heard by all present. Yet many of the needs that require intercession are private experiences of one person or perhaps a few. So when worship prayers include personal needs, the private become public. Therein lies the challenge. Sometimes the needs have already become public. But even then we ought to be sensitive to the fact that some worshipers have trouble with their needs becoming too public. I've had more than one parishioner come to me to explain their dilemma. One mother in particular expressed it well, "I am so grateful for a caring congregation and for the prayers in worship, yet as a rather shy and introverted person, I wince at the sudden loss of privacy. As a quite private person, it's difficult for me to know everyone is aware of my breast cancer. I feel like I'm blushing all the time." However we may answer her, the concern is a real one.

Our congregation was large, and receiving prayer requests from such a large crowd was challenging. In addition, the number of requests can be overwhelming. So we gave everyone a 3 x 5 card at the morning worship service and asked them each to write their prayer requests on it. We explained that all requests are legitimate; all will be remembered; and all privacy will be protected. At the close of the service all cards were collected and at the evening service all were spread out before the congregation on a table in front. The pastor prayed over all the cards, mentioning only the main categories of needs, assuming God had already read them all.

—A Pastor

Similarly, the question often arises of how much factual information we may share and when sharing runs the risk of violating privacy. This issue arises for both prayers and pastoral announcements. Should we just say that Andy has been hospitalized or that Andy has been hospitalized for the treatment of his depression? And should we say that Mary is having surgery, or may we say what kind if it involves her private organs? We can err on both sides: either to skip most information because it is too personal and delicate, or to include and run the risk of violating their privacy concerns. Resolving this dilemma will require trusting relationships with the people involved. We suggest efforts to seek their permission to share information. And we also encourage care to establish relationships that evidence our love for all so they can better understand our efforts in prayer. We walk a delicate balance between caring well for those who are in need, and not aggravating their needs by clumsy prayers.

The second area is that of *controversial issues*. On some issues we know there will be differences of opinion and conviction. Perhaps the community or the congregation is to vote on a somewhat controversial proposal; perhaps it's an election year; or some social issue is being debated. We are in a hard place. To pray specifically and realistically we might offend some worshipers, to pray in bland and vague generalities may risk really saying nothing. Yet to ignore or neglect the issue could condone inaction. Such may be the case in issues of justice, peace, poverty, political issues, and so forth. To avoid them makes a statement about our disengagement from key issues that impact our society, but to pray too specifically in some instances runs the risk of evoking conflict. As with laments (see chapter 21), the pain in such situations may need to be named, for our feelings are important to God, and we need to seek his guidance and help. But a prayer is not a campaign podium for a certain position. Wise is the worship leader who knows the difference.

The third area is that of *conflict within the community*. Every community—whether the congregation, the denomination, or the wider community—has conflict from time to time. Issues and questions arise that beg for resolution yet evoke strong reactions, sometimes with great heat. The issue may be a far-reaching one with large long-term consequences, or it may be a "tempest in a teapot." Or it may be personality or family differences. It matters not which it is. In situations like this, folks will carefully listen to how the leader prays for the matter and either how far from neutral the prayer came out or "what side" it emphasizes. For example, suppose that your form of church government places the authority for decision making in the hands of the governing board of the church, perhaps with consultation from the congregation, and now the church board is presenting a somewhat controversial proposal. The one who leads in the public prayers needs to be exceedingly cautious not to cross the line from praying for wisdom and discernment for all who will be making the decision, on the one hand, to praying for a certain specific outcome on the other hand. Perhaps it would be best to honestly state to God that while we face big issues we are having trouble agreeing with or accepting each other.

We can learn from the New Testament apostles, who faced such circumstances in the churches, particularly in the conflict between Jew and gentile and their differing religious practices. The apostles did not hesitate to take a firm stand where matters of right and wrong, ethical and unethical, justice and injustice were concerned. God's word and plan was at stake. But for the rest they focused on relationships with each other in the church. Uppermost in their prayers was the petition that brothers and sisters in the church would *behave* as brothers and sisters so as not to offend one another, thereby giving the world cause to reject the church and its witness. They seemed to be convinced that relationships are more important than some issues.

Public prayers say a lot about the church and about the Christian faith. They make a statement about God: he listens, he cares, and he gives us the right to openly and honestly share our concerns and needs with him. But such prayers also make a statement about the faith of the congregation: that we seek God's guidance, we are humbly committed to following him, and we value a relationship above all.

The congregation will be served well by worship planners and leaders whose stance in prayer is humble, caring, and courteous to all; who are knowledgeable and sensitive to those matters that might cause division unnecessarily; who are seasoned by loving relationships with worshipers enabling them to know the needs of all; and who are courageous enough to plead with God for matters of truth, justice, and righteousness.

TO PONDER AND DISCUSS

1. How many prayers are included in one of your normal worship services? Try to identify the purpose for each of them?

Make an assessment of how well each prayer fulfills that purpose?

2. How would you describe the way the pastoral prayers in your worship services treat privacy? Is there enough information so you know how to pray yet not so much that some are uncomfortable or offended?

3. After you have reviewed an audio or video record of your prayers in a worship service evaluate them with some of the thoughts of this chapter in mind? Then write a brief assessment to yourself of how sensitively you have handled challenging issues in prayer.

Chapter 23

When We Say Our Last Good-bye

SOMETIMES IT'S EASY FOR pastors to view funerals and memorial services as interruptions in their busy work week. They come unexpectedly, and often at inconvenient times. Most pastors will readily agree, however, that funerals and memorial services present some of the best opportunities for pastoral care. People are on the raw edge of life. They feel vulnerable. Often their confidence is shaken. They are asking questions of themselves that they do not normally deal with. What a golden time to come to them with the comfort, strength, healing, and hope of the gospel of Christ. Therefore, those who plan the services do well to give careful attention to such opportunities, even though they come at inconvenient times. And it seems appropriate that we include such events as one more part of caring liturgies the church provides, even though it may not be the weekly worship service.

Several audiences are likely to attend such events. First, are the primary grievers—those who most feel the sting of this event, because the deceased was a dear loved one. The death may have been anticipated, or it may have come suddenly and as a shock. Whichever, their hearts are heavy; they may feel numb; they are likely grasping for something safe, comforting, and secure, and they may even have some anger whirling inside their heart. They are usually the primary focus of our attention.

But the second group is that of extended family members who grieve with them and bring their own questions. Children and youth should not be overlooked. The loss of a grandparent, parent, or friend often creates confusion and opens their hearts to caring gestures and words. It may be their first encounter with death.

And the third group is composed of friends, neighbors, and associates. While some of these people may be able to minimize the pain, others are likely thinking of their own mortality and asking questions they haven't asked for some time, if ever. Perhaps some are uncertain about the Christian faith and need to hear the truth clearly and lovingly told. With such a diverse audience, those who lead will make their preparations with care and with a clear eye on each of these segments of the assembly.

The wise pastor, then, will carefully seek to communicate a spirit of caring that emphasizes three elements:

- life itself is sacred and to be held in high esteem as a gift from God;

- the physical body is sacred, created by God, and is to be treated with respect at all times;

- relationships are sacred and to be valued because they too are gifts from God.

Every person's story is significant, and therefore death is a time to retell the story so we are able to view this death in the context of the full story. Grieving is understandable and pain is natural when we see how this death has invaded a precious life story. As we trace the full story, therefore, we need to be directed to rest on the fact that only through the resurrection of Christ and our promised resurrection is there lasting hope for us, and only in God's purposes is the meaning of each story to be found. It will be meaningful, then, that when appropriate, we begin telling the story with a reference to the baptism of the deceased, the time when we received our identity in Christ.

Each culture legitimately develops its own unique practices to mark a death and to provide care for the mourners. In some settings burial happens quickly, within a day or two. In others, mourning begins with a visitation (a wake) and then a worship service, or in some cultures even daily worship services. Some prefer a funeral service, after which the family proceeds to the cemetery for a service of committal and burial. Still others prefer to hold a private burial service first and then gather with friends and family for a memorial service. Some will practice cremation, some not. In each instance the preferences of the family are important and the pastor will gently guide them in making their plans.

In the funeral or memorial service, several emphases should be in view to provide the proper care for those who mourn. First, we acknowledge the value of the person who died. This life story is sacred, though undoubtedly a mixture of pain and pleasure, good and ill. Such a life story is more comprehensive than a eulogy, which normally focuses on high praise for a person. While we tell the story we give thanks to God for his care and guidance in this life, which involve a mixture of success and failure.

Secondly, we acknowledge that grief and pain, even lament, are legitimate and may be openly expressed. Death is generally painful. Even when the circumstances have involved intense suffering, a final separation still involves pain. Sacredness has been violated, and relationships have been broken. Grieving is not a sign of weakness or of weak faith but a realistic response to the intrusion of death. In that sense it is better to acknowledge grief and pain than to hold a "celebration of life" that attempts to suppress all pain and sorrow. We remember how Jesus wept at the grave of Lazarus (John 11:35).

But third, and most importantly, we point to the death and resurrection of Jesus Christ as the sure ground of all our hope. Through the death and resurrection of Christ we have a sure ground for our eternal hope. Therefore the proclamation of the gospel of Christ is central to a Christian funeral service. We grieve, and it's OK to grieve, but we grieve as people who have firm hope!

Pastors and others who lead the gathered mourners do well to combine these three major motifs in such a way that the sad hearts of all who are present will find empathy, comfort, and, most of all, new hope.

Even when we are called upon to conduct a funeral service for someone who is not a Christian, our message to them ought to contain these three elements. Though we may not know the personal story of the deceased, we are wise not to assume things that we do not know about him or her. We are able to trace the story of their life from information gathered from the family; we can identify with them in their grieving; and we certainly can set the story of the Christian gospel before them. But we do so without words of judgment toward one who may not give evidence of being a believer, and without taking advantage emotionally of grieving family members in appealing for a decision on their part.

Generally, a graveside/burial/committal service is separate from a public funeral or memorial service. The quiet, somewhat more private, moments at a graveside are the time and place to offer special empathy, care, and hope. While it is often jarring to stand at a gravesite, the pastor's words should clearly point to our hope and comfort—that God can be trusted no matter what, even when we cannot understand the circumstances of this death. The act of committing the body to the grave is to be seen as a sure act of faith in the coming resurrection through Christ. In the same way, God, through Christ, can be trusted to guide us along the path ahead, even though it seems frightening and lonely from this vantage point. God will bring a final resurrection through Christ, even though this burial seems so terribly final. And God can handle all our doubts and questions as we try to process this whole experience.

A more opportune time for deep caring is hard to find. Wise are the pastors who seek to care well at such times.

The Structure of a Funeral or Memorial Service

1. We express our grief at the presence of death and the loss of this loved one through prayers, lament, songs, and Scripture passages.

2. We reflect on the story of this life and give thanks through Scripture passages, reflections by family and friends, songs, and prayers.

3. We proclaim and profess the gospel of Christ's victory over death through Scripture Readings, a message, and affirmations of faith and song.

Structure for a Graveside/Committal Service

Welcome and Invitation

Opening Readings of Scripture

The Words of Committal

> *Since God has called our beloved brother/sister from this life to himself, we therefore commit his/her body to the earth, for we are dust and to dust we shall return. But the Lord Jesus Christ will change our mortal bodies to be like his in glory, for he is risen, the first born of the dead. So let us commend our brother/sister to the Lord, that the Lord may embrace him/her in love and raise up his/her body on the last day.*

Prayer

Statement of Faith (such as the *Apostles' Creed)*

Benediction

—Leonard Vander Zee, *In Life and in Death*, 134.

TO PONDER AND DISCUSS

1. Recall a recent funeral or memorial service that you attended. What thoughtful pastoral care did you observe and experience in the service?

2. Funeral customs tend to change with each generation. What changes in funeral practices in your community today can you identify? Which changes do you view positively? Which do you find not so helpful?

3. What are some of the erroneous and unhealthy perspectives on death and funerals that you encounter in our society today? How do you feel about them?

4. Is it wise for Christians to pre-plan their funeral services with their loved ones and pastor? Why or why not?

Chapter 24

When We Marry

IT MAY SEEM STRANGE to you to find weddings included in this material about how pastoral care can be provided in the liturgy. A number of questions may immediately arise. Is a wedding a time of worship? Is the wedding service a liturgy? Surely pastoral care is provided in premarital planning with the couple, but can it also be present in the wedding liturgy?

Our answer to all of these questions is "yes" (ideally). Yes, a wedding is to be a time of worship. Yes, the wedding service is a liturgy. And yes, the wedding service is a setting for pastoral care. And yes, many of the same principles that guide us in worship planning will guide us in wedding planning also.

To be sure, these are counter-cultural answers. They are examples of how Christian worship and pastoral care contradict the standard practices and perspectives of our culture. To our prevailing culture, a wedding is not worship. It's a ceremony or a show perhaps, but not worship. And a wedding is not a time for pastoral care. It's a time for a legal transaction and public affirmation of a relationship perhaps, but not pastoral care. You've probably encountered that.

How are we able to make a case for pastoral care in a wedding service? We are assuming, of course, that a pastor is presiding at the wedding ceremony. And we are assuming that the pastor understands this role as a servant of Christ. And we are assuming this is a Christian wedding. So let's examine some of the considerations in this matter.

The pastor's first concern should be the spiritual commitments of the two who are being married. The pastor has the responsibility to marry only those who are "marrying in the Lord," a clear reference to the words of Paul in 2 Corinthians 6:14, as well as other places, which call for both marriage partners to possess a "common commitment to the Lord of life," as a marriage formulary expresses it. Therefore, in conversations with the potential bride and groom, the pastor will have addressed this matter as a part of pastoral care for them. This commitment will also become public in the wedding ceremony.

But other considerations will also determine whether and how much pastoral care is offered. Think of these considerations:

1. *Investing in the couple.* Investing ourselves in the lives of others is an act of loving service. Pastors exhibit their care for an engaged couple when they refuse to stay at a distance, but give of themselves personally in planning, preparation, mentoring, and instruction for those to be

Weddings in which two families are to be blended are a special challenge, for the families and for the officiating pastor. When Gary and Mae were married, seven grown children were involved, and all were committed to successfully blending their families and to making a public commitment to that hope in the wedding.

After the bride and groom exchanged their vows, the bride was asked to receive the groom's children and treat them as her own, and the groom was asked to receive the bride's children as his own.

When the bride and groom had taken their vows, all seven children came forward. His children took vows to receive their new mother with love and respect. Her children promised to receive their new father with love and respect.

The entire family formed a circle of prayer for God's blessings on their new relationships.

—Used with permission

married. A pastor is not a stranger to the bride and groom, but a friend. This invested relationship becomes the setting in which pastoral care can be provided.

2. *Structuring the marriage ceremony.* A pastor who is lovingly committed to this new couple will not avoid the hard work of carefully planning the marriage ceremony. No invested pastor will say, "Whatever you plan is fine. Just let me know what you want." Valuable pastoral care will be received when a pastor works carefully with them to piece together all the elements of a God-centered ceremony. A caring pastor will guide in the selection of appropriate songs, Scripture passages that will allow the voice of God to be heard, prayers that will express the Lordship of Christ in marriage, our need for the grace to be faithful, vows that are biblical, a challenge to live obediently before God, and a benediction that expresses God's continued presence with them. A pastor may want to put special attention on the blessing of and parting from their parents as the ones whom God has used to prepare these two for this day. The pastor may also incorporate a reminder of their baptisms as the day they received their identity from God, an identity they now will be living out in the marriage relationship.

3. *Crafting a memorable message.* A wedding is obviously not the place to expect folks to listen well to an extended sermon. The distractions are many, their minds are on other things, and the wedding party is usually standing. Yet where is there a better opportunity to speak clearly and engagingly the truth about marriage? To do so well, however, the pastor will have to prepare a crisp, easy-to-understand, and memorable message for the occasion. This is not the time for off-the-cuff frivolous comments, but rather a time for warmly and clearly speaking of love, commitment, covenant-keeping, and grace.

4. *Remembering the secondary audience.* While the wedding and its message are primarily for the bride and groom and their families, those who are guests at a wedding are certainly

not just spectators. They have been invited because they have some special relationship with the bride and groom. They will likely be asked to take a vow to support and pray for the new couple, a commitment they must take seriously. The better they understand this vow, the better they will appreciate the ways in which we all need a community to support us in our marriages. And while the pastor may not have personal acquaintance with many of the guests, it is safe to assume that many can benefit from the same instruction the bride and groom receive. Among them will be children and youth whose values need to be shaped by such experiences, and perhaps some whose love has grown cold, whose sights need to be reset, or who are traveling some difficult parts of their journey. They too need reminders of the vows that were once taken often require a recommitment.

In such instruction, the truth must come through that sometimes the best pastoral care that can be provided comes through the counter-cultural message that a Christian wedding is worship, the service is a liturgy, and all that we say and do in vow-taking and celebrating is before the face of God. Wise is the pastor who willingly accepts that role. And blessed is the couple who is cared for lovingly and thoughtfully by such a pastor.

Jon and Laura were a groom and bride who were conscious of their baptismal identity as Christians and understood that they would begin their married life as two baptized people. So they desired that their wedding ceremony begin at the baptism font. They joined the officiating pastor at the font, splashed the water, and recalled that water cleanses, purifies, refreshes, and sustains, and that Jesus Christ is the living water. The pastor invited them to renew their baptism vows, and they did so before all who were present. Having completed this remembrance of their baptism, the bride, groom, and pastor moved to the center of the platform and proceeded with the wedding and its vows.

—Used with permission

TO PONDER AND DISCUSS

1. Do you agree that a wedding should be a time of worship and not merely a ceremony? What are your reasons for your convictions about that? Do most of the weddings you have attended fit that description? What is the role of our culture in shaping what a wedding is and ought to be?

2. What other ways, besides those mentioned here, can you think of in which an officiating pastor can provide pastoral care at a wedding?

3. Cite three or four marks that ought to characterize a Christian wedding.

Bibliography

Anderson, Bernhard H. *Out of the Depths: The Psalms Speak to Us Today.* Philadelphia: Westminster, 1983.

Dawn, Marva. *How Shall We Worship? Biblical Guidelines for the Worship Wars.* Wheaton, IL: Tyndale, 2003.

"The Heidelberg Catechism." In *Our Faith: Ecumenical Creeds, Reformed Confessions, and Other Resources.* Grand Rapids: Faith Alive Christian Resources, 2013.

The Holy Bible, New International Version. New York: International Bible Society, 1978.

Kidd, Reggie. *With One Voice: Discovering Christ's Song in our Worship.* Grand Rapids: Baker, 2002.

Lift Up Your Hearts: Psalms, Hymns, and Spiritual Songs. Grand Rapids: Faith Alive Christian Resources, 2013.

Neville, Gwen Kennedy, and John H. Westerhoff III. *Learning through Liturgy.* New York: Seabury, 1978.

Plantinga Jr., Cornelius. *Beyond Doubt: Faith-Building Devotions on Questions Christians Ask.* Grand Rapids: Eerdmans, 2002.

Revised Common Lectionary. Minneapolis: Fortress, 2005.

Reinstra, Debra, and Ron Reinstra. *Worship Words: Discipling Language for Faithful Ministry.* Grand Rapids: Baker, 2009.

Vander Plaats, Dan, and Elim Christian Services. "The 5 Stages: Changing Attitudes." 5 Stages: The Journey of Disability Attitudes. www.the5stages. com/wp-content/uploads/2013/10/The5Stages_2014.pdf (accessed Nov 7, 2016).

The Worship Sourcebook. 2nd ed. Grand Rapids: Calvin Institute of Christian Worship and Faith Alive Christian Resources, 2013.

Webber, Robert. *Worship Is a Verb.* Waco, TX: Word, 1985.

Willimon, William. *Worship as Pastoral Care.* Nashville: Abingdon, 1979.

Yancey, Phillip. *Disappointment with God.* Grand Rapids: Zondervan, 1988.

Vander Zee, Leonard. *In Life and in Death: A Pastoral Guide for Funerals.* Grand Rapids: CRC, 1992.

Made in the USA
Middletown, DE
09 May 2019